GREATEST
WONDERS
OF THE WORLD

IN ASSOCIATION WITH
TIMPSON

GREATEST
WONDERS
OF THE WORLD

AARON MILLAR

Published in the UK in 2016 by
Icon Books Ltd, Omnibus Business Centre,
39–41 North Road, London N7 9DP
email: info@iconbooks.com
www.iconbooks.com

Sold in the UK, Europe and Asia
by Faber & Faber Ltd, Bloomsbury House,
74–77 Great Russell Street,
London WC1B 3DA or their agents

Distributed in the UK, Europe and Asia
by Grantham Book Services, Trent Road,
Grantham NG31 7XQ

Distributed in Australia and New Zealand
by Allen & Unwin Pty Ltd,
PO Box 8500, 83 Alexander Street,
Crows Nest, NSW 2065

Distributed in South Africa by
Jonathan Ball, Office B4, The District,
41 Sir Lowry Road, Woodstock 7925

Distributed in India by Penguin Books India,
7th Floor, Infinity Tower – C, DLF Cyber City,
Gurgaon 122002, Haryana

Distributed in Canada by Publishers Group Canada,
76 Stafford Street, Unit 300, Toronto, Ontario M6J 2S1

Distributed in the USA by Publishers Group West,
1700 Fourth Street, Berkeley, CA 94710

ISBN: 978-178578-124-7

Images – see individual pictures

Typeset and designed by Simmons Pugh

Printed and bound in the UK by Clays Ltd, St Ives plc

For my wife Gillian, and our wee family:
truly the greatest wonder of all

ABOUT THE AUTHOR

Aaron Millar is an award-winning travel writer. He contributes regularly to *The Times*, the *Guardian*, *National Geographic Traveller* and many other national and international publications. He has presented travel documentaries for National Geographic and is the 2014 British Guild of Travel Writers Travel Writer of the Year. He grew up in Brighton, England and at the time of writing is hiding out in the Rocky Mountains of Boulder, Colorado.

For more about Aaron, visit www.thebluedotperspective.com

'Aaron Millar has a great way with words and knows how to bring a place and story to life. A pleasure to read.'
Jane Dunford, Travel Editor, *Guardian*

'Aaron Millar's travel writing is, quite simply, among the best there is. Both lyrical and informative, it is a joy to read.'
Jane Knight, Travel Editor, *The Times*

CONTENTS

Europe

Middle East

Africa

Asia

Oceania

Arctic/Antarctica

Outer Space

INTRODUCTION

Wonder is fine dining for the soul. There is no other animal on Earth, as far as we know, that can marvel at the planet like we can, that feels awe and humility, that is moved to tears by the sheer beauty of a sunset or the magnificence of the stars at night. Wonder is what makes us who we are. It drives us to explore, question and connect. And it is that impetus, to fill the world with all the possibilities of our imagination, which has carried us so far. Wonder is the pure joy of being alive. But we must nourish it for it to thrive. If this book aspires to one thing, it is this: live life to the full, celebrate your world and feed your spirit well.

Each wonder in this book is superlative in its own right: the largest, deepest, tallest, most audacious, beautiful, complex and awe-inspiring things on the planet. Some are man-made, some are natural; there are wildlife spectacles and human spectacles too. Many have never been included in a major compendium before. These are wonders not just of our past, but our future, too: the Large Hadron Collider, the most complicated machine ever built; the International Space Station, the greatest international peacetime collaboration in history; the Rio Carnival, the biggest party on the planet.

I hope to take you on a journey. I want you to feel what it's like to stand beneath the sweaty heat of the tallest waterfall on the planet or float on your back on the deepest lake in the world, 5,000 feet of darkness screaming up beneath you. I want to walk you up the freezing face of the tallest mountain on Earth; I want you to see 30,000-year-old cave paintings by our primitive ancestors and hear the thunder of a million wildebeest chasing rainbows across the Serengeti. Each wonder has a unique story to tell, each has mysteries hidden within.

But this is not just a list of sights; it's also a road map for discovering the greatest experiences of your life. I hope you'll travel with me: from your armchair, your commuter train, the pillow propped up on your bed. I hope you'll feel something of that spark of wonder as you read this book. But I also want to give you all the information that you'll need in order to follow that spark from these pages into the world for real. So, at the end of each chapter, I'll also tell you the best ways to visit these wonders for yourself and reveal the insider tips that will help you get the most out of your experience. From how to hear the 'sound of infinity' in the Taj Mahal to where you can swim up safely to the thundering edge of Victoria Falls.

Socrates said 'Wisdom begins in wonder'. Studies have shown that awe creates empathy and altruism; that it helps us connect with others and the world around us in meaningful and lasting ways. The experience of wonder is not just a fleeting passion; it is a seed from which the best things in life grow. And that's important. Because the more you look for wonder in the world, the more the wonder of the world becomes a part of you.

Wonder transcends all boundaries, nationalities and beliefs. It is a conduit to our past, our future and a sense of something greater than ourselves. It is the stuff that makes life worth living. But most of all, wonder is inside us, every time we look in awe at the world and realise that we are a part of that world too. Explore, dream and feed your soul well.

THE 50 GREATEST
WONDERS OF THE WORLD

NORTH AMERICA

BRISTLECONE PINES, CALIFORNIA

Bristlecone Pines are the oldest living organisms on Earth. When the first stones of the Great Pyramids were being laid, Methuselah – the name given to what is perhaps the most ancient of these trees at more than 4,800 years old – already had its roots in the ground. They pre-date the birth of Christ, the fall of Troy, the invention of the alphabet.

But these remarkable trees are more than just gnarled wood and endurance. Written in the rings of their twisted, wind-battered trunks are the chronicles of their long life. And discovering those stories has led to surprising breakthroughs in our understanding of climate change, forest ecology and even the history of our own civilisation.

Adversity is their friend. Should they be nurtured with water and shelter they simply grow faster and die young. But give them an arid climate, exposed to the wind and cold, one that is too harsh for insects, disease and competition from other plants, and they will simply go on indefinitely. The oldest grove, where Methuselah itself is found, is more than 10,000 feet up in the parched White Mountains of California. Living branches are covered in thick green needles, which themselves survive for a staggering 40 years. The trees grow squat, to no more than 60 feet. As they age they thicken instead, spinning with each inch to strengthen their grain. And no two are alike. Each one has been whipped smooth

Photo: Rick Goldwasser

by the endless scour of windswept sand and ice, like skeletal sculptures twisting up from the earth.

But it's the tenacity with which they cling to life that is most impressive. Scientists have recorded trees, entirely encased in dead wood, with less than 10 per cent still alive. A tiny sliver of bark connected to root will sustain a Bristlecone for centuries. And despite often being more dead than alive, the living parts of even the oldest trees have the health and vitality of newborns. Peer into their rings and the wood they produce on their thousandth birthday is as fresh and untainted by age as a sapling. Even in death they can remain standing for millennia.

But despite Methuselah's prodigious age, it is not, in fact, the oldest tree that has ever been recorded. That now infamous story belongs to a young geographer, who in 1964 while taking core samples got his borer stuck in a tree. To retrieve it, and salvage his research project, he cut it down. That tree, now named Prometheus, he later discovered, was around 4,900 years old, meaning he simultaneously found and killed the oldest living thing in the world.

But however inspiring it is to be in the presence of such antiquity, in the end it's what we're taught that matters most. Dead Bristlecone Pine wood can remain intact in the cold, dry climate of the White Mountains for thousands of years. Using a combination of living and fallen trees, scientists, beginning with Edmund P. Schulman, who discovered Methuselah in 1957, have now pieced together a continuous tree-ring chronology that extends back almost 10,000 years – to the end of the last ice age. Because the trees tailor their growth to temperature, their rings are like a thermometer frozen in time. By reading between the lines, literally, we can glimpse into the environmental conditions of our past and uncover patterns of climatic change that may help us predict the future. And it's not all good news: over the last 50 years Bristlecone rings have grown fatter than at any other time in the last 3,700 years. Our world, according to these old trees, is rapidly warming.

Bristlecone Pines are also known as the tree that rewrote history. For many years, scientists have used a technique called radiocarbon dating to establish a timeline for archaeological events. But the process needed calibrating. By correlating the amount of carbon-14 in samples of individual Bristlecone tree rings with existing radiocarbon data, scientists discovered that many previous historical estimates were wrong. Ancient artefacts found in Europe turned out to be 1,000 years older than previously thought; established theories of cultural diffusion were suddenly refuted; the development of civilisation itself was redrawn.

But perhaps we shouldn't be surprised at such wisdom. Bristlecone Pines were here when the first Native Americans spread across the continent; they stood sentinel to the rise and fall of Rome, Greece and the Incas. To be near them is to touch the resonance of that deep longevity with our own hands – as if our fingers might grasp a concept our minds could never fully comprehend. But they ask questions of our future too. The weathered old Pine that was a mere sapling when the Pyramids were built lived to see the atom split and man walk on the moon. But what of the tree that is just now taking root? What new secrets will be written, 5,000 years from now, in the rings of the oldest living thing on Earth?

WHERE: Ancient Bristlecone Pine Forest, White Mountains, California.

HOW TO SEE IT: The identity of Methuselah is kept secret in order to protect the tree from damage, but it can be found, along with dozens of other ancient Bristlecones, 10,000 feet up, somewhere in the Schulman Grove. For the best view, hike the four-mile Methuselah Trail from the Grove car park. Don't miss the Patriarch Grove as well, an otherworldly landscape of moon-like rock and desolate trees, eleven miles (and 1,500 feet in altitude) further up a dirt track. www.fs.usda.gov/main/inyo/home

TOP TIP: Come at dusk when the setting sun makes the tannins of the trees glow bright red, orange and amber.

TRY THIS INSTEAD: The most ancient trees are found in California, but at more than 3,000 years old the Bristlecone Pines at Great Basin National Park in Nevada are no spring chickens either. A three-mile hike leads to a spectacular grove nestled on the side of Mount Wheeler. www.nps.gov/grba/index.htm

THE GRAND CANYON, ARIZONA

There are few landscapes more inspiring and worthy of wonder than the Grand Canyon. At 277 miles long, a mile deep and up to eighteen miles wide, this kaleidoscopic red rock gorge of the Colorado River is nature at its most dramatic, humbling and unfathomably large. The poet Harriet Monroe called it 'the abode of gods. It made a coward of me'. To stand on its rim is to grasp, in an instant, the insignificance of our short lives and, yet, the unimaginable beauty to which we bear witness.

It's not the biggest canyon in the world. Tibet's Yarlung Zangbo Grand Canyon is more than 30 miles longer and more than three times as deep. There are gorges in Peru whose walls would tower above it. But it's surely the most spectacular. Amber rock spires rise up from the snaking Colorado River like stone totems. Brush-stroked cliffs of gold, orange and crimson shift with shadows and the changing mood of the day. Everything is stripped bare – like peering into the sinews of the Earth. At dawn, silence sullens the pink temple-buttes. At dusk, the rocks glow like embers of a great fire. This is a landscape of myths, as big as giants, too vast and uncontained to be real. On a clear day you can see for 100 miles and still only take a fraction in. And the more you look, the more you feel like you might simply float away.

But what makes this canyon Grand is more than just enlightening views. Written within its sheer 5,000-foot walls is the most complete geologic record on the planet. Nearly 2 billion years of natural history, close to 40 per cent of the Earth's entire lifespan, is engraved in these narrow cliffs – from the formation of the first life forms, through the evolution of plants, fish and amphibians, to early mammals and finally us. It's like a photocopy of time itself, a panorama of the past etched into stone.

But the Grand Canyon itself is a relative newbie. The Colorado River began carving into the bare rocks of the Colorado Plateau about 6 million years ago, descending 2,000 feet in its journey through the Canyon, gathering speed and tearing up boulders that scoured the exposed chasm like a knife. In times of extreme flood the river flows at 300,000 cubic feet per second – the equivalent of a skyscraper of water rushing through the gorge every single minute. At the close of the last ice age, as the glaciers were melting in the Rocky Mountains, there might have been three times that force.

As the river cut down into the Earth's crust, it exposed layer upon layer of much older rocks, gradually revealing

the tapestry of geologic time that we see today. From the Kaibab limestone at the top, laid down some 260 million years ago by an inland sea, through sandstone and shale to granite and Vishnu schist, formed 1.8 billion years ago, and now exposed at the river's bed. Each layer tells its own story: desert becomes sandstone, mud becomes shale, the skeletons of sea animals harden into limestone. Reading into the rocks we can see oceans advance and retreat, mountains rise and fall, deserts form and disappear. Fossils are everywhere: 500-million-year-old ocean-dwelling trilobites, footprints of scorpions, centipedes and dragonfly wings. But no dinosaur bones: even the most recent of these old stones were laid down before their time.

And there's more than just rocks too. Within the Grand Canyon National Park there are sandy beaches and emerald pools, waterfalls and rapids surrounded by hanging gardens of honey mesquite, orchids and coyote willow; above the desert scrub and cacti, there are swathes of sagebrush and juniper and then higher still rich forests of ponderosa pine, spruce-fir, aspen and oak. Five of America's seven life zones are stepped into the Canyon's mile-high elevation.

There's history too. The first Westerner to set eyes on the Grand Canyon was the Spaniard García López de Cárdenas in 1540. John Wesley Powell survived a three-month ordeal rafting through it in 1869. But the true discoverers of the Canyon were the Native Americans who lived here for thousands of years before Europeans arrived. Petroglyphs colour the chasm walls, there are food stores cut high into the cliffs, 2,000-year-old split-twig figurines – willow branches carefully folded into animal shapes – have been found placed ceremoniously in remote caves. The oldest artefacts here date back almost 12,000 years – a continuous record of human habitation. Even the walking paths we use today were once native hunting trails and the two biggest tribes, the Hualapai and the Havasupai, still reside on reservations in and around the Canyon. For them, it is a sacred place. And it's become a sacred place for us too.

The writer J.B. Priestley said that the Grand Canyon is not 'a beauty spot, but a revelation'. Some landscapes leave an imprint on the soul. The Grand Canyon is the abode of the gods, a chronicle of deep time, a view that may just change your life.

WHERE: Grand Canyon National Park. The South Rim entrance is about 70 miles north of Flagstaff, Arizona.

HOW TO SEE IT: The south rim is where 90 per cent of visitors go, so escape the crowds at the remote north rim, 44 miles south of Jacob's Lake, or by hiking, rafting or taking a mule trip into the canyon itself – a unique perspective that few visitors get to see.
www.nps.gov/grca/index.htm

TOP TIPS: One of the best places to watch the sunset is Hopi Point, but in the summer months it can get crowded. For a less congested view try Yaki and Pima Points on the south rim instead. On the north rim, many rangers recommend Point Imperial for a breathtaking, and crowd-free, sunrise.

TRY THIS INSTEAD: Antelope Canyon, just two hours north of the Grand Canyon in the Navajo Reservation, is one of the most spectacular slot canyons in the world. At the start and end of the day, the swirling red, pink and bright orange colours of the rock are mesmerising. Use an authorised Navajo guide to explore inside the narrow canyon walls.
www.navajonationparks.org

MAUNA LOA AND KILAUEA, HAWAII

Mauna Loa is the largest active volcano on Earth. Located in Hawai'i Volcanoes National Park, on the 'Big Island' of Hawaii, its gentle slopes belie its staggering enormity. More than 60 miles long and 30 miles wide, taking up roughly half of the island, it fills approximately 19,000 cubic miles of solid rock – 3,200 Mount St Helens could fit within its enormous frame. From sea level it rises to 13,680 feet, but its flanks continue underwater for a further 16,400 feet, and then depress the sea bed a further five miles down. The total height of Mauna Loa, from the start of its eruptive journey to its crater, is roughly 56,000 feet – almost twice the height of Mount Everest.

And it's still active. Since 1843 there have been 33 eruptions. The last was in 1984 when lava flows reached within four miles of the town of Hilo, forcing many residents to evacuate. When that happened, molten magma seeped through cracks in the Earth's crust and fireworked into the air, iridescent rivers of fire drained like spilt honey to the sea. Over the last 3,000 years Mauna Loa has erupted roughly every six years. She's been taking a nap for the last 30 years or so, but not for long.

The entire region is part of the Pacific Ring of Fire – a 25,000-mile band of intense seismic and volcanic activity stretching from the south-western tip of South America, upwards along the North American west coast and across to the eastern edges of Asia and Australia. Within its belt there are thought to be 452 volcanoes – the most active and deadly ones in the world.

But however big Mauna Loa is, or impressive her eruption will one day be, her sister still steals the show. Kilauea, just

25 miles east, is widely regarded as the most active volcano in the world. It's been erupting near continuously since 1983 – one of the longest running eruptions in history – and has covered nearly 40 square miles of the island in its lava flow. Right now, as you read this, it is more than likely bubbling an enormous cauldron of fire like some giant witch's brew.

Or more accurately, a goddess. Legend has it that Kilauea's smouldering crater is the home of Pele, the Hawaiian goddess of volcanoes. In local dialect her name is 'Ka wahine 'ai honua', the woman who devours the land. Eruptions are an expression of her fiery temper, and her longing to be with her love. But beware of the curse: it is said if you remove volcanic rocks from her island home, she will inflict bad luck upon you. Whether you believe the legend or not, hundreds of pieces of lava rock are mailed back to the island each year from travellers who claim to have suffered misfortune since they took a souvenir home.

But volcanoes are more than mere destruction. They are creators too. More than 80 per cent of the Earth's surface above and below sea level was formed by volcanic activity. Hawaii's islands are themselves the product of countless volcanic eruptions – and Kilauea and Mauna Loa are adding landmass to the chain every year. Gas from ancient eruptions may also have been instrumental in forming the first molecular building blocks of biology. Their fires may have warmed the primordial soup.

Volcanoes are testaments to the origin of the Earth. But they are also a reminder that those same forces are still shaping the planet today. The world is in a constant state of flux. Cycles of violence and creation have been spinning for aeons and will continue to do so long after we're gone. Mauna Loa and Kilauea are windows into the inner workings of the

Photo: Hawaii Volcano Observatory, USGS

world – the largest and most active volcanoes on Earth, side by side, like sisters, fiery goddesses that will roar again one day.

WHERE: Hawai'i Volcanoes National Park, Big Island, Hawaii.

HOW TO SEE IT: Take the Crater Rim Drive, or Chain of Craters Road, for the best lookouts into the Kilauea crater and other volcanic hot spots in the park. Then, if conditions permit, arrange for a private guide to show you where the lava flows into the Pacific Ocean – one of the most spectacular ways to see the world's most active volcano at work. For a true adventure camp at the summit cabin of Mauna Loa, but be prepared for a long hike, unpredictable weather and altitude sickness. The Mauna Loa Trail and the Observatory Trail are two of the most popular ways up. Register at the Kilauea Visitor Centre before setting off. March to November is the best season.
www.nps.gov/havo/index.htm

TOP TIPS: Come at night to see Kilauea's crater fire bubbling in the dark. Check the Hawaiian Volcano Observatory website for regular updates on Mauna Loa's eruption status.
http://hvo.wr.usgs.gov

TRY THIS INSTEAD: Iceland is one of the most volcanically active countries on Earth, with regular eruptions roughly every three to four years, some of which can be observed first hand. Or for something a little different, try going into a volcano itself. Thrihnukagigur Volcano has a hollowed out 400-foot deep magma chamber and is the only volcano in the world that you can explore inside.
www.visiticeland.com
www.insidethevolcano.com

METEOR CRATER, ARIZONA

Fifty thousand years ago a pinpoint of light appeared in the sky above what is now northern Arizona. Passing through the Earth's atmosphere it grew into a brilliant fireball, brighter than the sun, hurtling towards the ground at 26,000 mph – more than 30 times the speed of sound. The meteorite weighed 300,000 tonnes and was more than 150 feet across. As it struck the Earth it exploded with a force greater than 20 million tonnes of TNT – 1,000 times more powerful than the atomic bomb that destroyed Hiroshima. Shock waves swept across the plain, levelling forests and flinging mammoths, giant sloths and mastodons through the air. The ground melted instantly on impact. Earthquakes rippled across the land. A dense cloud of molten hot iron, nickel and burning pieces of rock rained down like a fiery mist.

This meteor crater may not be the largest in the world: that honour belongs to Vredefort Crater in South Africa, at 186 miles across, and more recently a still-to-be-confirmed discovery in the Warburton Basin of Australia, at 249 miles across. But most craters erode and gradually disappear over time: Vredefort is best seen from space, the Australian impact site was detected underground. This one is different. The high desert landscape that surrounds the crater has preserved the impact site in near perfect condition. It's like watching that moment of destruction, frozen in time.

The size alone is staggering. The crater reaches 550 feet deep, the equivalent of a 60-storey building, and over 4,000 feet wide. But perhaps most remarkable of all is the fact that somewhere underground there are microscopic fragments of rock and metal that originated in the depths of space. Being here is awe-inspiring, but a little frightening too. Asteroids

Photo: Daverosolis

have bombarded the Earth for aeons, and will continue to do so. Scientists estimate that dozens pass closer than our moon, undetected, every year. In 2015 one enormous, 1,800-foot wide killer passed within 300,000 miles of Earth – a hair's breadth in astronomical terms. The question is when, not if, a meteor will strike again.

But the crater is impressive for other reasons too. Its story begins when a local miner named Daniel Barringer heard tales of an enormous cavity in the Earth where pieces of metal could be found. Up to that point the scientific community were convinced the crater was caused by a volcanic eruption. But Barringer was beset by the idea that underneath that giant hole was a meteorite that contained enough iron to make its finder one of the richest men in the world. From 1903 to his death in 1929, he drilled, experimented and rallied the scientific community around his theory. But to no avail. It was only in 1960 when planetary scientist Eugene M. Shoemaker discovered two rare forms of silica on the site, coesite and stischovite, both of which do not occur naturally on Earth and can only be created through exposure to extremely high pressure, that Barringer's theory was finally vindicated.

It was a groundbreaking moment in scientific history, the first time a meteor crater had been conclusively discovered on Earth. It helped explain the large round craters that had been observed on the moon. It weighed in on theories about the extinction of dinosaurs, and became a vital stepping-stone in trying to understand the dynamic interplay of gradual and cataclysmic forces that have shaped our planet.

And Barringer's Crater is still aiding scientific discovery today. NASA astronauts use it for training. Interplanetary robots test their mettle on its rocky curves. And, by examining the gullies caused by erosion, it's teaching scientists how to better search for water on Mars.

But, perhaps, most amazing of all is just being there. To see, with your own eyes, the unfathomable forces that forged our world. To touch a direct line to the stars. Barringer's Meteor Crater is a stark reminder of the awesome power of the universe and our own fragility within it. Look up: you never know, that pinpoint of light might be hurtling towards us again soon.

WHERE: Near Winslow, northern Arizona.

HOW TO SEE IT: Take the guided rim tour for the best views and background on the impact site.
www.meteorcrater.com

TOP TIP: Stick around after the sun sets for dark skies and world-class stargazing.

TRY THIS INSTEAD: Wolfe Creek National Park in Western Australia is home to the second largest meteor crater in the world where fragments of a meteorite have been collected. It's also been extremely well preserved. Only accessible in the dry season, May to October, 93 miles south of Halls Creek via the Tanami Road.
https://parks.dpaw.wa.gov.au/park/wolfe-creek-crater

GIANT SEQUOIAS, CALIFORNIA

The General Sherman Tree, a Giant Sequoia found in the southern range of California's Sierra Nevada Mountains, is the largest living thing on the planet. At 52,500 cubic feet it's big enough to hold a concert for more than 2,000 people and still have enough room to wiggle. It weighs 2.7 million pounds. It stands 275 feet tall. Its branches can reach seven feet in diameter. Its bark can be more than two feet thick. It would take eighteen people linking fingertips at full stretch to circle it. They call it the General for a reason: it commands respect.

But General Sherman is just one tree. The Giant Sequoias themselves are the real wonder. John Muir, the legendary environmentalist and founder of the Sierra Club, called them 'the God of the woods'. Dark reddish-brown bark, blanketed in branches of evergreen needles, stretch up hundreds of feet, from a thick base to a bushy crown. They are the colossi of the living world. To walk among them is to have your neck craned, your ego levelled and your eyes filled with awe.

But there's not many left. Vast forests of Giant Sequoias, and their cousin the Redwoods – often confused, but distinct and equally impressive trees – once covered the entire northern hemisphere. The oldest known fossil records date them back to the time of dinosaurs. They look like giants because they come from a time of giants. To stand beneath them is to be dwarfed not just by their size, but by another era entirely.

Now Giant Sequoias can only be found along a thin 260-mile long, 15-mile wide corridor on the western slope of the Sierra Nevada. They are prodigious growers, but they are picky, requiring just the right amount of heat and cold to survive. Truly enormous trees, like General Sherman, also require thousands of gallons of water each day. Since the Sierra generally has dry summers this moisture is provided from the snowpack that accumulates higher in the mountains over the winter months and then soaks into the ground in spring. In this narrow band of life, usually between 5,000 and 7,000 feet in height, there is enough snowmelt to provide ample water, while at the same time not being too high and too cold in winter, nor too low and too warm in summer.

They owe their enormous size to their resilience. They are simply too big to blow over. Their thick bark is rich with tannins, which helps protect, and insulate, them against fire, insects and disease. And should a branch or two get burnt off, they have the unusual ability to simply sprout a new one. As much as 95 per cent of a Giant Sequoia's foliage can be decimated through fire and yet they can carry on growing for centuries. Which they do: many of the largest living Sequoias today are thought to be between 2,000 and 3,000 years old. Muir called them: 'near immortal' and he was nearly right. They're big, simply because nothing can take them down.

But their greatest threat today is man. Native people lived among these trees for more than 8,000 years without cutting a single one down. Then, in the mid-19th century, the gold rush came. The first official record of a Sequoia sighting was in 1852 by Augustus T. Dowd. That old tree, now named the Discovery Tree – the remains of which can still be seen in Calveras Big Tree State Park – was cut down a year later. Its stump was so large that it was used as a dance floor. Historical sketches depict couples in ball gowns and tuxedos prancing improbably on top of an enormous felled tree. But, thankfully, the wood of these giant trees was generally too brittle for full-scale construction projects and by the 1920s the logging of Giant Sequoias had largely stopped.

But a new threat has now emerged. Giant Sequoias are on the front line of climate change. Drought, increasing temperatures and decreasing levels of snowpack are all bad news for these forest giants. If we don't act quickly the next generation of colossi may never crane our necks and fill our eyes with wonder.

Photo: Alberto Carrasco Casado

WHERE: Sequoia & Kings Canyon National Park, near Fresno, California.

HOW TO SEE IT: The Giant Forest, a grove of Sequoias set within the national park, is the home of General Sherman and offers the best access to the biggest trees – including five of the ten largest on the planet.
www.nps.gov/seki/index.htm

TOP TIP: When photographing the giant trees, put a person in the frame to give the image a sense of scale.

TRY THIS INSTEAD: Coastal Redwoods, otherwise known as Giant Redwoods, are an equally impressive tree species. While Sequoias are the largest by volume, Redwoods are the tallest – with the current record standing at about 380 feet tall, or roughly the equivalent of a 35-storey building. They also require very specific climatic conditions and exist only in a narrow band along the Pacific Coast where coastal fog and a humid climate act like steroids on their growth rate. See them at Redwoods National and State Parks, and other reserves, along the Californian coast.
www.nps.gov/redw/index.htm

YELLOWSTONE GEYSER BASIN, WYOMING, MONTANA AND IDAHO

Covering 2.2 million acres of Wyoming, Montana and Idaho, Yellowstone, founded in 1872, is America's first national park and the inspiration for wilderness preservation everywhere.

Grizzly bears, wolves, elk and bison make their home here. It is one of the last great wildernesses on the continent, a symbol of the boundless freedom of the old American West, and part of one of the most intact temperate ecosystems on Earth. But what makes Yellowstone a wonder of the world has nothing to do with that. It's what's happening below ground that counts.

In the early 19th century, when the first mountain men and fur trappers began returning from the far reaches of the still wild west, they brought stories home of a magical landscape where the Earth bubbled and giant fountains of boiling water exploded into the air. They were dismissed out of hand as myth. But following expeditions later that century, the reports were confirmed. Yellowstone really was magic. In fact, it's the largest active geyser basin on the planet. There are more than 10,000 hydrothermal features here, including the world's biggest concentration of geysers, more than 300, as well as the highest density of hot springs, mud pots and steam vents anywhere on Earth.

Old Faithful, named by early explorers for her clockwork eruptions every 90 minutes or so, is the star of the show: a giant plume of superheated water that erupts as much as 180 feet into the air. But its fame rests on its reliability. Giant Geyser nearby can reach 250 feet, but is infrequent. Steamboat Geyser, in the Norris Basin, is the world's tallest with eruptions up to 300 feet, but during its long dormant periods you may have to wait decades to see it.

But, in truth, the real wonder of Yellowstone is no particular feature by itself, but the geyser basin as a whole. Within the two square miles of the upper section alone there are nearly one-quarter of all the geysers on Earth. Thermal jets shaped like beehives and castle turrets, spouts that bubble like fountains or shoot like guns into the air. Walk around and you'll find super-heated pools of pure sapphire, boiling pots of gloopy, cinnamon coloured mud and scorching water tapestries of green, amber and gold.

Near to Old Faithful and the geyser basin is the Grand Prismatic Spring, the largest hot spring in the USA: dark blue, cyan and turquoise waters, 370 feet wide, ringed by layered lines of yellow, orange and deep red like a rainbow fallen to Earth. And then 50 miles further north is another wonder, the terraces of Mammoth Hot Springs, where mineral-rich water, heated deep underground, rises through cracks in the Earth and solidifies into multi-coloured travertine sculptures, like an enormous abstract art installation.

The aesthetics are mind-blowing, but what's truly amazing is that all these thermal worlds are alive. Microscopic bacteria and algae, called thermophiles, thrive in these extreme conditions, creating vivid colours as they feed in distinct, narrow bands of heat. Blue for archaea – an entirely new kingdom of life, discovered in the late 1970s, surviving at 93°C; yellow for bacteria at 75°C; green, algae at 60°C; orange, protozoa at 56°C. These are the artists of Yellowstone. They are among the most prevalent and least understood organisms on Earth. But they are helping us to solve some of the greatest mysteries of our time.

The key to unlocking the DNA code was discovered basking in Yellowstone's lower geyser basin. Viruses discovered in Yellowstone's thermal waters are helping in the fight against Aids, Ebola and other diseases. Advances in climate change science and oil and gas extraction are credited to Yellowstone's microbial world. And we are only just beginning: it is estimated less than 1 per cent of Yellowstone's thermophilic potential has been discovered.

But the greatest discovery of all may not even be on this planet. Astrobiologists from NASA, the people charged with finding out whether or not we are alone in the universe, are

Photo: Flicka

studying Yellowstone's extreme environments in order to better help them search for life elsewhere in the universe. By studying life in these extreme conditions, which mirror those of Mars, Europa and other planetary bodies, they can figure out what real extra-terrestrial beings might look like. Far from little green men, many scientists think they may look a lot like Yellowstone's geyser basin. That would be a story: the most alien environment on the planet helps to find the first alien environment off the planet.

But we may have to act quickly. Firing all this geothermal energy, just a few miles underground, is one of the largest active volcanoes in the world. The last time it erupted, 640,000 years ago, it was 1,000 times more powerful than the 1980 eruption of Mount St Helens. When, not if, it goes again, it will decimate the country and cover half the world in darkness and ash. For all its wonder, Yellowstone is a ticking bomb.

But that's also what makes it so special. Written on the walls of Old Faithful's visitor centre is a quote from the American painter Anne Coe, who called it 'the place where the centre of the earth finds an exit and gives us a glimpse of its soul'. This is the planet at its most primal, the birth of creation itself. It's more than just the largest geyser basin in the world; it's a glimpse into the engine of the Earth. And, perhaps, a peek at our future too – here and beyond the stars.

WHERE: Yellowstone National Park, Wyoming, Montana, Idaho.

HOW TO SEE IT: All of the major thermal features have raised boardwalks that are easy to navigate. But try getting off the main thoroughfare too: many of the remote geysers are only a short hike away.
www.nps.gov/yell/index.htm

TOP TIPS: Yellowstone in summer is crowded. Come in winter to have the geyser basin all to yourself. Download the NPS Yellowstone Geysers app to plan your visit around predicted eruption times.

TRY THIS INSTEAD: Rotorua, on the North Island of New Zealand, is also one of the largest geothermal areas in the world and filled with many of the same spectacles, colour and wonder as Yellowstone.
www.rotoruanz.com

CENTRAL AMERICA

CHICHÉN ITZÁ, MEXICO

The ancient Mayans are one of the most remarkable civilisations the world has ever seen. Without the wheel, or advanced tools, they managed to build elaborate stone pyramids and temples in the middle of the jungle. The first written language of the Americas was introduced by them. They independently developed the concept of zero centuries before India, China and the ancient Greeks. And their knowledge of astronomy was simply stunning: using only the naked eye, their observations of the heavens match up to the measurements of modern science today. And then suddenly, without warning, they disappeared. What happened to the ancient Mayans remains a mystery, but the remnants of their remarkable civilisation remain.

The ancient city of Chichén Itzá, which thrived between

AD 750 and 1200, is not the biggest Mayan archaeological site in Mesoamerica – Caracol in Belize is more than 30 times as large and the pyramids of Tikal in Guatemala dwarf it. But it is, perhaps, the most astounding, for written within its ruins is the pinnacle of Mayan, as well as their equally impressive neighbours, the Toltecs', thought and culture. It is one of the best preserved of their great cities, or Tollans: a masterpiece of ancient architecture produced by one of the most fascinating cultures in world history.

The site itself, a jungle-kissed plateau in Mexico's northern Yucatán peninsula, is 740 acres of ornate temples, structures and columned arcades, interconnected by a dense network of paved pathways called *sacbeob*, or white roads. At the heart of Chichén Itzá is El Castillo, the spectacular Pyramid of Kukulkán, named after the legendary ruler of the city. Its four steep 79-foot walls rise up to an intricately carved temple on its summit where the most important religious ceremonies were performed. Buried inside archaeologists have found the remains of an even earlier pyramid too, where a snarling jaguar throne with jade eyes stares out from the darkness inside.

Nearby is the Temple of the Warriors, flanked by rows of pillars and statues of feathered serpents and the Osario Step Pyramid. But perhaps the most impressive part of the whole city is the observatory. Astronomy was central to Mayan existence. They believed that the sun, moon, planets and stars were gods and that by tracking their movements they could better understand divine influence upon the Mayan people. As a result, they spent much of their resources carefully charting the paths of celestial bodies and their degree of accuracy is astonishing. Using only the naked eye astronomer-priests were able to predict solar eclipses and equinoxes with pinpoint precision. They calculated the length of a year to be 365.242 days; modern measurements put it at 365.242198. The orbit of Venus was predicted to within two hours of a 584-day cycle. Their measurement of the lunar month differed from ours by less than nine seconds. Astronomy fuelled the growth of their culture, helping them to advance their agriculture, create calendars and develop highly sophisticated measurements of time.

Indeed, Chichén Itzá itself was built according to these profound astronomical observations. Each side of the great pyramid has 91 steps, add in the top step to the temple and that equals 365, one step for every day of the year. The number 91 is also the number of days that separate the seasonal phases of the solar cycle: spring, summer, autumn and winter. The pyramid itself would have acted as a kind of calendar with the interplay of light and shadows signifying key agricultural and ceremonial times of year. Indeed, one of the greatest spectacles of the entire region occurs at each spring and autumn equinox when the sun casts a shadow in the shape of a giant serpent that moves down the pyramid's steps to align with an enormous sculpture of a snake head at the base of the temple.

But astronomy wasn't their only achievement. They built complicated looms for weaving cloth; they produced the first rubber products 3,000 years before Goodyear received his patent; they established trade routes as far as South America and mastered complex farming and irrigation systems in even the most inhospitable of locations. And their written language was the most advanced in the region: an intricate system of about 800 different symbols, each one corresponding to a different syllable or word, which can be combined in almost infinite ways. Breaking the Mayan code took 200 years and was one of the greatest achievements of modern archaeology.

Given these astonishing achievements it would be easy to assume that the ancient Mayans were a peaceful people – philosopher kings more intent on deciphering the mysteries of the cosmos than chopping off each other's heads. But nothing could be further from the truth. War was a way of life at Chichén Itzá – and the violence extended inside the city walls as well as out. North of the Great Pyramid lies a series of sinkhole wells where victims were thrown in alive to appease the rain god. At the summit of the Temple of Warriors it's possible to touch the altar where they used to rip out the still beating hearts of sacrificial victims. And right in the centre of the city is Chichén Itzá's great ball court, the largest in Mesoamerica. Here players would attempt to throw a rubber ball, often stuffed with a human skull inside, through one of four twenty-foot high stone rings on each of the surrounding four walls. The stakes were enormous: the vanquished lost their heads as well as the game.

But however bloodthirsty their practices appear to us today, their achievements seem all the more remarkable for it. Inventors, astronomers, master builders: Chichén Itzá is more than just old stones; it's a testament to human ingenuity, intellect and imagination.

WHERE: Yucatán, Mexico.

HOW TO SEE IT: Day trips are organised from numerous popular resorts, including Cancún. But for the best experience stay overnight in one of the nearby towns. You'll be the first on site and will avoid the afternoon heat and day-tripper crowds. Plus it's a great chance to experience some of modern Mayan culture too.
www.chichenitza.com

TOP TIP: To watch the shadow of the snake phenomenon, come the week before or after the equinox instead of the actual date itself. The crowds are a fraction as large and the spectacle is almost as good.

TRY THIS INSTEAD: Tikal in Guatemala is equally impressive, more atmospheric and has fewer visitors. www.tikalnationalpark.org

MONARCH BUTTERFLY MIGRATION, MEXICO

The migration of the Monarch butterflies is one of the most astonishing journeys in the animal kingdom. Every autumn tens of millions of Monarchs travel from eastern Canada, across the USA, to their winter hibernation grounds in the Transvolcanic Mountains of Mexico. It's a journey of between 2,000 and 3,000 miles. For a creature that weighs half a gram, and measures about four inches, that's a preposterous distance. The comparative trip length for a 150-pound human would be more than 300 million miles – or roughly 700 round trips to the moon.

But the length of the journey is only part of the wonder. The truly baffling fact is that they do it across multiple generations, without a guide and without ever having been there before. The butterfly that departs from Canada will die before returning home. And so will its offspring. It will be left to the fourth generation, the great granddaughter of that original butterfly, to begin the migration anew next autumn. How millions of Monarchs find their way across a continent to the same specific twelve mountains every year,

Photo: hspauldi

having never been there before and with no guide, is still one of the great mysteries of the natural world.

Their journey begins at the end of summer. Drops in temperature, the angle of the sun and dwindling food sources activate certain genes within the Monarch's DNA that drive physiological changes, preparing the butterfly for its long journey ahead. Monarchs born at this time are entirely different from their mothers and grandmothers: their muscles are more efficient, their metabolic rate changes, they begin to store fat and lose the ability to mate. These are the migratory generation – the superheroes of the butterfly world. They live eight times longer than their parents or their offspring and travel ten times as far. The sole purpose of their existence is to reach the hibernation grounds in Mexico, survive the winter, and then mate so their offspring can complete the cycle.

They fly four to six hours a day, gliding between thermals for 20 to 30 miles, sometimes reaching thousands of feet in the air. Along the way they must avoid seas and storms, seek shelter from the cold and thread a geographical needle between river valleys and mountain ranges, in order to hit a roughly 50-mile gap that will take them to the specific forests where their great-grandparents roosted a year ago.

How they complete this amazing feat of navigation was a mystery for many years, but science now has some answers. In part they simply use the sun – their brains have a powerful in-built compass that is orientated towards the sun. Even on the cloudiest days they can lock on to it through the polarisation of light. The problem is the sun moves across the sky during the day. They can't just be following it blindly; something else is required. Recent studies have revealed that the Monarch's antennae also have an incredibly sensitive biological clock. That means they can correlate the relative position of the sun to the time of day. In effect, their brain is like a powerful time-compensated sun-compass. Just like Boy Scouts are taught to use their watch and the sun to find their way, Monarchs, by combining the information from their eyes as to where the sun is with the circadian rhythms in their antennae as to what time of day it is, can always find south.

But that only solves one mystery. At a crucial point in their journey they turn due east to reach their overwintering grounds. That means they must somehow know where to go, and when to turn, even though they've never been there before and no one's showing them the way. And the Monarchs begin from multiple locations and are able to adjust their route as required. They're not just following a compass heading, they're actively navigating a route as they go. No one has a conclusive answer to how this is done, but it is thought that it is some type of genetic memory – a kind of inherited GPS-like software with a pre-programmed destination built in.

Their arrival, usually around mid-October, is spectacular: millions of golden black butterflies cover the branches of the evergreen and oak forest like a thick orange coat, huddling together for warmth during the long winter. Locals once believed they were the angels of their ancestors coming home to visit because they usually appear around the Mexican Day of the Dead. Then, in spring, after their long hibernation, the mountains are filled with fluttering wings and a frenzy of activity as the super generation of migratory butterflies prepares to fly again. But this time for only about as far as southern Texas, where they stop to mate, lay eggs and die. It will take two more generations, each one living for only six weeks, to relay the final leg of the journey and somehow make their way back to a home they've never been to before.

It's one of the most astonishing journeys in the animal kingdom, but it's getting harder each year. Illegal logging of their overwintering grounds and the use of harmful pesticides on their primary food source, milkweed, across the Midwest USA is continuing to decimate their numbers. Where once a billion butterflies took to the skies, now just a fraction of those numbers have survived. For a creature that is used to hard journeys, the longest road may be just ahead.

WHERE: Reserva de la Biosfera Mariposa Monarca (Monarch Butterfly Biosphere Reserve), Michoacán, Mexico.

HOW TO SEE IT: El Rosario, 129 miles west of Mexico City, is the largest and most accessible area of the reserve but still involves a steep climb to reach the observation points. Hire a local guide with a horse for an easier route up. Sierra Chincua, near the town of Angangueo, is another popular area.
www.visitmexico.com

TOP TIPS: Avoid crowds of local day-trippers by visiting on a weekday. Come in February, and time your visit with a sunny day, for the most activity.

TRY THIS INSTEAD: A number of Monarch butterflies also spend the winter in southern California. Though smaller in number, it's still a spectacular sight. See them November through February at Pismo Beach Monarch Grove in San Luis Obispo County and Goleta Monarch Grove in Santa Barbara.
www.monarchbutterfly.org
www.goletabutterflygrove.com

MOSQUITO BAY, PUERTO RICO

The water in Mosquito Bay, Puerto Rico, is like liquid stars. Swish your hand through it and neon blue lights will follow behind like the tail of a comet. Splash an oar and an entire world of luminescent sparks will dance on the surface. Schools of fish pass underneath like glowing disco lights. Waves shimmer with electricity. This small inlet on the southern shore of Vieques Island, eight miles off the coast of Puerto Rico, is the best place in the world to see one of nature's most spectacular, but lesser known, wonders: bioluminescence.

Mosquito Bay's starry waters are caused by a special kind of photosynthesis-using plankton called *Pyrodinium bahamense* dinoflagellates, or dinos for short. When dinos become agitated, they respond by flashing a blue-green light as a defence mechanism. These one-celled organisms measure only about 1/500th of an inch, but the burst of light they give off is 100 times bigger than they are and easily perceived by the naked eye. In a gallon of water there are roughly 700,000 dinos and the effect is impressive; in the ocean it's spectacular.

But it's also incredibly rare. Bioluminescence occurs spontaneously across the globe, but there are only six bays in the world where the phenomenon can be seen regularly. Of those, three are in Puerto Rico. But Mosquito Bay, also known as Bio Bay, is the best, holding the Guinness World Record for the brightest bioluminescence ever recorded. The reason has to do with the precise conditions in which dinos thrive. The bay is small and shallow, with a narrow mouth, preventing them from being washed out to sea. It is surrounded by mangroves, which provide vital nutrients. The water stays

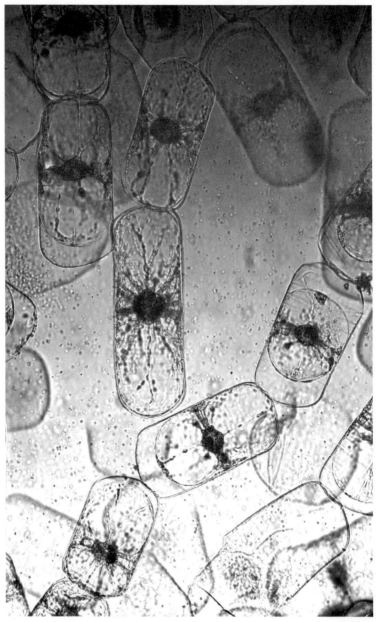

Photo: Narrissa Spies

warm, and calm, throughout the year, allowing saltier water to sink to the bottom and get flushed out of the bay.

Limited human contact has helped too. For 60 years Vieques Island was the test ground for the US Navy until they pulled out in 2003, under pressure from the local population. As a result Mosquito Bay was spared development. Other bays haven't been so lucky. La Paguera, on the Puerto Rican mainland, has dimmed to near extinction from exposure to chemicals in boat fuel and pollutants on the skin of swimmers. Vieques is now growing in popularity. To keep this wonder shining bright, tourism is now strictly monitored and controlled, but the fate of the bay remains to be seen.

And it's important we keep these remarkable ocean fireflies safe, because they have a lot left to teach us. Although bays like this are rare, bioluminescence itself is not. In fact it's the primary communication tool of the deep ocean, used for everything from attracting a mate to warding off predators. It is one of the oldest fields of study too. Aristotle was the first to record detailed observations of bioluminescent creatures, including dinos, which he prodded with a fishing rod in order to watch them glow. Christopher Columbus referred to mysterious lights in the sea. And a young Charles Darwin marvelled at the luminosity emitting from the wake of the HMS *Beagle*.

The study of bioluminescence, in more modern times, has heralded radical breakthroughs in medical science too. A green fluorescent protein, found lighting up the bodies of a particular species of jellyfish, is now used by doctors as a kind of glow-in-the-dark torch into the molecular world. By attaching that protein to certain cells they can literally illuminate processes that had hitherto been invisible. Work is also underway to use bioluminescence to better map brain processes and help in the fight against cancer. But the future may bring more surprising developments too: research is being conducted to see if bioluminescent trees can be created to replace energy-draining streetlights, it's been suggested we may one day engineer crops that glow when they need water, bright bioluminescent sweets are not far from our supermarket aisles.

For now, though, perhaps it's enough just to be there, to see those living lights respond to your touch, to have the cosmos mirrored in perfect reflection. In a world where everything can be viewed at the click of a button, Mosquito Bay is unique. Videos don't do it justice. Photographs are poor imitations. You have to see it with your own eyes.

WHERE: Mosquito Bay, Vieques Island, Puerto Rico.
www.vieques.com

HOW TO SEE IT: Kayak tours are the best way to see the phenomenon, but electric boat tours are also available. Book with a licensed guide to help protect the bay.

TOP TIP: Time your visit with a new moon for the best viewing conditions.

TRY THIS INSTEAD: Laguna Grande bio bay in Las Croabas, Fajardo, on the Puerto Rican mainland, near the capital San Juan, is easier to get to and still offers a spectacular show. Or for an alternative bioluminescent experience try the Waitomo Caves on New Zealand's North Island. Thousands of glow-worms light up the cave walls like stars.
www.seepuertorico.com
www.waitomo.com

SOUTH AMERICA

THE AMAZON RAINFOREST

The Amazon rainforest is the largest tropical rainforest on Earth. This vast expanse of almost 400 billion trees is nearly twice as big as India and more than twenty times the size of Great Britain. It covers 2.1 million square miles of Brazil, Peru, Ecuador, Bolivia, Colombia, Venezuela, Guyana, Suriname and French Guyana – roughly 40 per cent of the entire South American continent. If it was a country, it would be the ninth largest in the world.

But size is only part of its wonder. The Amazon is the most biodiverse place on the planet. Ten per cent of the world's known species live here – including an estimated 2.5 million types of insects, most of which have never been recorded. Twenty per cent of the world's oxygen is produced by its forest. One fifth of the world's fresh water is stored in its basin. The Amazon rainforest is more than a precious eco-system, it is the lungs and life force of the planet itself.

At the heart of the forest is the Amazon River. Stretching more than 4,000 miles from the Peruvian Andes across the northern half of South America to the Atlantic Ocean in Brazil, it is the largest river by volume in the – ten times greater than the Mississippi and more than four times bigger than the Congo, the second largest on the list. It drains an area close to 3 million square miles, which collects an average of nine feet of rainwater a year. In the summer, snowmelt from the mountains raises the water level by more than 30 feet to flood the forest basin for twelve miles inland from the main channel.

The volume of that cumulative amount of water is staggering. Twenty-eight billion gallons of fresh water flow into the Atlantic every minute. Its daily discharge would be enough to supply New York City's fresh water needs for nine years. That immense pressure pushes the river 125 miles out to sea before it mixes with the saltwater of the Atlantic. Early sailors could drink freshwater straight out of the ocean before even setting sight on land.

And where the river flows, it breathes life. The Amazon is home to more than 420 types of mammals, 1,300 species of birds as well as hundreds of reptiles and amphibians. There are snakes that weigh 500 pounds, which could eat you whole, Jesus Lizards that can walk on water and glass frogs with translucent skin. And most of the Amazon is still undiscovered – we know less about the canopy of the Amazon rainforest than of the ocean floor.

And that's why it's so precious. Twenty-five per cent of all prescription drugs derive from ingredients found in rainforests, yet only 1 per cent of tropical plants have been studied for their medicinal potential. Cures for Aids, cancer and diseases we haven't even encountered yet are more than likely growing, right now, somewhere in that vast fertile basin. The Amazon is the medicine cabinet of the world and we've barely opened the door.

The keepers of this knowledge are the indigenous tribes that have lived there for thousands of years. The Amazon is the ancestral home of 1 million native Indians, from more than 400 tribes, each with their own distinct language, knowledge and culture. Many of those tribes have still never made contact with the outside world. There are people

living in these forests today who have absolutely no idea of the universe beyond the trees.

But their world is shrinking. Industry is eating away at their territory at a staggering rate. Without any written language, if a shaman dies before passing on his knowledge, the accumulation of thousands of years of medicinal information comes irreversibly to an end. It's like burning libraries. And the destruction is coming fast. In the time it's taken you to read this chapter, more than 500 acres of Amazon rainforest will have been cleared. Two football pitches are lost every second. To date more than 20 per cent has been converted to raising cattle, settled or used in mass-scale farming, mining and logging.

Those practices not only endanger the planet, they miss the true potential of the forest. One acre of timber yields an owner roughly US$60. One acre for grazing approximately $400. But that same space used for renewable medicinal plants and fruits can yield more than $2,400. The future security of the Amazon may lie in realising its economic value for science.

But facts and figures are only part of the story. The Amazon is as essential to our survival as the air we breathe. But to see it first hand offers something else too. It is a living testament to the infinite creativity of evolution. To be here is to glimpse the vast, and barely comprehended, interconnectedness of life, to realise in an instant how fantastically bizarre and amazing this world really is, and how we're a part of it.

WHERE: Sixty per cent of the Amazon rainforest is found in Brazil. Peru has roughly 13 per cent and Colombia 10 per cent. The rest is spread out between Ecuador, Bolivia, Venezuela, Guyana, Suriname and French Guyana.

HOW TO SEE IT: Manaus in Brazil is a common gateway to the Amazon. But Bolivia offers an excellent, and often less crowded and cheaper, experience too. The wet season is February to April, the dry season is September to November. Come in the dry season for hiking and May to June for river activities.
www.visitbrasil.com
www.bolivia.travel

TOP TIP: Small boat river cruises and indigenous operated eco-lodges are some of the best ways to see the Amazon.

TRY THIS INSTEAD: Costa Rica's Oso Peninsula has spectacular old growth rainforests and is a good budget alternative.
www.visitcostarica.com

MACHU PICCHU, PERU

The ancient stone citadel of Machu Picchu is one of the most breathtakingly beautiful archaeological sites in the world. Built by the Incas in the 15th century, this dramatic complex of 200 stone temples, homes and sanctuaries is perched 8,000 feet high in the Andean jungles of Peru and stretches across more than 80,000 acres of tropical mountain top. The site is magnificent, circled by three sacred peaks, or apus, and surrounded by the Urubamba River and the Amazon rainforest below. At dawn the ancient ramparts float above the morning mist like a lost city in the clouds.

The rise of the Incas was spectacularly quick. At its peak, their empire stretched from the capital Cuzco in

Photo: Allard Schmidt

southern Peru across the western edge of the Andes from Colombia in the north through Ecuador, Bolivia and Chile to the tip of Argentina in the south. One single ruler, Topa Inca Yupanqu, is credited with expanding their reach by an astonishing 2,500 miles in just over twenty years. They flourished for little more than a century, from 1400 to their conquest by the Spanish in 1533. But in that brief flash they managed to construct a road network of more than 14,000 miles, subjugate over 10 million people, speaking more than 30 different languages, and become the largest civilisation of its time anywhere in the world. They built many cities during their reign, but Machu Picchu was their crown jewel.

Their work was stunning. The entire complex blends into the natural surroundings with exceptional harmony of design – as if it is an extension of the mountain itself. But it was also well made. Without iron or steel, the Incas used hard stones from the river to chip away at the white granite quarried on the mountain summit. They had no mortar so carved precisely shaped interlocking bricks instead, simply balancing one on top of the other. And their craftsmanship was so exquisite that to this day, 500 years later, a knife still can't be inserted between the blocks.

They had foresight too. In order to provide food for the population, they built over 700 terraces cut into the mountainside, where maize and potatoes would be grown. To feed this agriculture they needed a reliable source of water. So they built a system of highly advanced aqueducts that carried natural sources through the city via a complex series of canals and fountains. But the terraces also acted as a defence against landslides, literally gripping the city to the steep slopes. The foundations were constructed with multiple layers of topsoil, gravel and waste rock that aided in the drainage too. Without that forward thinking, 79 inches of rainforest downpours a year would have simply washed the city away.

The purpose of Machu Picchu, in such a remote and inaccessible location, was a mystery for many years. But it's now believed to have been a kind of royal retreat for the great warrior king Pachacuti Inca Yupanqui, the ninth ruler of the Incas. But it was also a sacred site and religious ceremony would have played a key role. The Incas worshipped the sun, moon, stars and planets and many of the buildings at Machu Picchu were constructed according to these astronomical functions. At summer solstice, for example, sunlight shines through a window of the Temple of the Sun, one of the most beautiful buildings of the entire complex, and aligns perfectly with a boulder in its centre and a nearby sacred peak. Nearby, the Intihuatana stone, a carved monolith to the west of the main plaza, would have functioned as a kind of solar clock and helped plan the timing of religious ceremonies. The truly remarkable thing is that the Incas managed to do all this and more without written language, or even the wheel, in the middle of one of the densest jungles on Earth.

But Machu Picchu is more than just the sum of its parts. In his diary, American explorer Hiram Bingham, the first Westerner to discover it in 1911, called it 'an unbelievable dream'. That description is as apt today as it was more than 100 years ago. It is a place of awe and magnificence, a marvel of engineering and design. Here, perhaps more than anywhere else on Earth, nature and the vision of mankind blend seamlessly into something more powerful, and more beautiful, than each would be on its own.

WHERE: Urubamba, Peru.

HOW TO SEE IT: April to November is the best time of year,

but avoid the busy months of June and July, when crowds are at their greatest. The majority of people travel from Cuzco to the nearest town Aguas Calientes and then take the train up from there. It's essential to buy permits in advance. Tickets can be purchased at the official office in Cuzco or online at www.machupicchu.gob.pe. For something more adventurous, try the 26-mile Inca Trail, but altitude, steep climbs and extreme weather make it a challenging trek. And it's packed: 75,000 people make the journey each year. Consider trying one of the alternative routes instead, such as the Lares or Salcantay Routes.
www.peru.travel

TOP TIPS: Get there for sunrise and stay for sunset. Hike up to Huayna Picchu for the best views of the site.

TRY THIS INSTEAD: Choquequirao is located nearby in Peru's Sacred Valley. It's smaller and less dramatic, but receives a fraction of the visitors and is well worth a look.

ANGEL FALLS, VENEZUELA

Angel Falls is the highest free-falling waterfall on the planet. Pouring out of an immense flat-topped mesa, called a tepui, deep in the Guiana Highlands of South-east Venezuela, its total height is 3,212 feet – including a spectacular single drop of 2,647 feet. If you were standing on top of the Empire State Building in New York City, you wouldn't even reach halfway up this enormous cascade. Rivals are babes in its presence. The Angel is nine times taller than Victoria Falls in Southern Africa, eleven times more elevated than Iguaçu in Brazil, and fifteen times the height of Niagara in the USA. By the time the water reaches the Kerep River, at the base of the mountain, it has fallen so far that most of the flow is vaporised into a sheer mist that can be felt a mile away.

The indigenous people of the region, the Pemón, call her 'Kerepakupai-Meru' – 'the waterfall of the deepest place'. The name Angel comes from the first Western man to see it, an American aviator named Jimmie Angel, and his story is almost as spectacular as the waterfall itself. Legend has it that he was once a World War combat ace for the Royal British Flying Corps, that he helped a Chinese warlord create an air force in the Gobi Desert and worked as an aviation scout for Lawrence of Arabia. But legend also has it that Jimmie liked a good story.

What is undeniably true is that he was a gifted pilot and spent much of his life working in remote regions of Central and South America looking for gold, diamonds and oil. In the 1920s he met an American mining geologist, named McCracken, in a bar in Panama, who agreed to pay him $5,000 to fly to a remote location in Venezuela. The pair landed on a tepui mountain top and pulled a fortune in gold from a river on that plateau. Jimmie would spend the rest of his life trying to find that fabled lost river again. Indeed it was while searching for it in 1933 that he caught his first glimpse of Angel Falls. Convinced his lost river of gold may be feeding that enormous cascade, he returned soon after with his wife Marie and two Venezuelan guides to explore the top of the mountain.

But disaster struck. After two days of searching it was clear there was no gold and, in the meantime, his plane had become hopelessly stuck in the mud. They had no choice but to abandon the plane and begin a treacherous

Photo: Rafael Estrella

eleven-day trek down from the remote plateau. The romance of that extraordinary adventure, which they all survived, captured the world's attention. *National Geographic* sent Ruth Robertson, an American photojournalist, to document the falls in 1947 and she returned with spectacular images and a precisely recorded height. Soon after, famed Latvian explorer Aleksandrs Laime cut a trail through the dense jungle to become the first Westerner to approach the falls on foot. Scientists and researchers followed in their dozens thereafter.

What they found was remarkable. It turns out the tepuis are as much a natural wonder as Angel Falls itself. Towering 9,000 feet into the clouds, with sheer rock cliffs and thick, untouched jungle on their summits, these geological phenomena are like islands in the sky – completely disconnected ecosystems that have evolved independently from the world around them. The Pemón believe the spirits of the dead reside there. Arthur Conan Doyle imagined a lost world where dinosaurs and prehistoric beasts still roamed free. The truth is almost as fantastic: entirely new species of plants and animals, which exist nowhere else on Earth, are still being discovered on these remote mountain tops. Even now, there are creatures wandering around up there that the world has never seen.

That's what makes Angel Falls special. It's still wild. It's still an adventure. No one knows exactly what's on top of the jungle that feeds it. In a world where satellite can look into every corner, and the internet brings even the farthest reaches of the planet into our front rooms, there is something comforting in the knowledge that there are still unexplored corners left. There are adventures still to be had, wonders to fly past. Jimmie would have approved.

WHERE: Canaima National Park, Venezuela.

HOW TO SEE IT: Fly to Canaima from Caracas via Ciudad Bolívar or Puerto Ordaz. Book a guided trip from there, usually involving a four-hour boat ride up the river and then a hard 90-minute hike.
www.salto-angel.com

TOP TIP: The flow of the falls lessens considerably in the dry season. Come June to September for the best views, though be prepared for clouds and delays.

TRY THIS INSTEAD: Iguaçu Falls on the Brazil–Argentina border is a jaw-dropping series of 275 individually linked falls. Come in spring or autumn to see it at its best.
www.visitbrasil.com

THE GALÁPAGOS ISLANDS, ECUADOR

The Galápagos Islands are the greatest wildlife show on Earth. This tiny archipelago, 600 miles off the coast of Ecuador, is home to more than 9,000 species and has the highest level of endemism anywhere on the planet. Giant tortoises, flightless cormorants, marine iguanas and unique species of penguins, fur seals and sharks can be seen here and nowhere else in the world. But biodiversity is only part of it. What makes the Galápagos truly special is that all these animals are utterly fearless of human contact.

Isolation has protected them. Aside from a few buccaneers and whalers from the 17th century onwards, human

Photo: David Adam Kess

interaction has been close to non-existent for most of the islands' history. Even now, 97 per cent of their landmass is a protected national reserve. As a result, people are not seen as predators; they're a curiosity. Mockingbirds perch on your shoulder, sea lions swim up to play; it's possible to walk through enormous breeding grounds of Waved Albatross and be as invisible as the breeze. The Galápagos are more than just a wildlife spectacle, it's a glimpse of the world untainted by human touch.

The nineteen islands of the Galápagos chain were first discovered by the Dominican friar Fray Tomás de Berlanga, the Bishop of Panama, in 1535, after currents inadvertently set his ship off course on the way from Panama to Peru. In the 17th century pirates such as William Ambrose Cowley, who drew up the first navigational charts of the islands, used the Galápagos as a base to plunder Spanish galleons laden with New World gold. Here they would stock up on fresh water and easy meat: Giant Tortoises, who could live for a year without food or water, were kept alive in their holds, stacked brutally upside down on their shells. But it is the voyage of the HMS *Beagle* that put the islands on the map.

When Charles Darwin set sail on his five-year exploratory journey around the world, serving as a naturalist and gentlemen companion on Captain Fitzroy's ship, he was 22 years old. He had some experience collecting small specimens of insects and sea creatures, but was otherwise a complete novice of natural history. The *Beagle* arrived in the Galápagos on 15 September 1835. They stayed six weeks and Darwin spent nineteen days ashore, collecting specimens and making observations. Later, when he returned home to England, he began to wonder how it's possible that one island could have its own unique species – animals that could be found nowhere else on the archipelago – if the climatic and environmental conditions of the entire region were near identical.

The prevailing view of the time was that plants and animals were immutable, created through a divine act. In his book *On the Origin of Species*, published in 1859, Darwin proposed a radical alternative. His observations of Galápagos species, including the famed Darwinian Finches, proved the high level of endemism found on each island. But at the same time it showed the close interrelatedness of those species to neighbouring islands. Rather than assuming that each of these variations constituted a unique species, Darwin argued that they are in fact the same species that had diverged over time due to minute behavioural differences. Living things were not created whole, he proposed, but rather were constantly adapting to their environment. Natural selection. The survival of the fittest. We don't just exist, we evolve.

This simple idea explained all of life and its consequences and set a course for natural science that we are still following today. The Galápagos may barely register on a world map, but this minute archipelago in the middle of the Pacific Ocean has changed the way we think about life, and ourselves, more profoundly than anywhere else on the globe. The Galápagos Islands are more than just the best wildlife show on Earth: they are a glimpse of the world before human contact and the seed of one of the greatest ideas of all time.

WHERE: The Galápagos Islands, Ecuador.

HOW TO SEE IT: Most people visit the Galápagos on organised cruises. Another option is to stay ashore and take day trips to nearby sights. Although often more cost effective, the range of islands that can be seen is usually less.
www.galapagos.org

TOP TIPS: December through May is the rainy season. Expect bright sunshine, temperatures in the high 20s(°C), warmer oceans and less choppy seas. This is the best time to see birds mating. June through November is the dry season. Temperatures cool, seas get rougher and the water colder, but there's less rain and many animals become more active. This is the best time of year for diving and snorkelling. Invest in a good telephoto lens – at least 200 mm – or, if you can afford it, a pair of image stabilising binoculars.

TRY THIS INSTEAD: There's nowhere quite like the Galápagos. But Ecuador's cloud forest is a bird lover's paradise and, because it's only a few hours away from Quito, the initial port of entry for most travellers, it can easily be combined with a Galápagos trip.
www.ecuador.travel

THE NAZCA LINES, PERU

The Nazca Lines are one of archaeology's greatest enigmas. These enormous etchings, or geoglyphs, were scratched from the surface of the Earth, by hand, more than 1,500 years ago. Located 280 miles south of Lima, on the arid coastal plains of Peru, the more than 300 drawings depict a range of animal and humanoid shapes as well as complex geometrical patterns: jaguars, sharks, decapitated heads and strange supernatural beings. The largest is a bird, 990 feet long; there is a 600-foot lizard and a carved white monkey that's longer than a football pitch. They scatter 290 square miles of the brown and barren desert like a vast art installation.

Nazca people spent centuries perfecting these etchings. Yet, to this day, no one knows exactly why they did it. Some argue they're part of a complicated astronomical calendar, or match patterns in the sky, still others dream up elaborate religious ceremonies or complex irrigation systems. Whatever the purpose, the drawings are astonishingly precise for such large works. And, most baffling of all, they are best viewed from the air – though the Nazca would have had no way of knowing that or appreciating such a view for themselves. Who they were drawn for, and why, remains one of the world's great mysteries.

The geoglyphs were created by removing red stone pebbles from the dusty plateau in order to expose the white gypsum subsoil underneath. It took generations: superimposing, overwriting and reinterpreting older drawings one on top of the other like scribblings on a blackboard. And they've stood the test of time. These large flat plains, or pampas, of southern Peru are one of the driest and most windless places on Earth, helping to preserve the Lines in almost the exact condition in which they were first created.

The Nazca thrived here for centuries, clinging to slivers of green river valley, flowing down from the Andes. They produced beautiful ornate pottery; they grew cotton, beans and corn and built cities. They were a remarkably green society: farmers planted seeds with a single hole in order to better preserve the soil; they recycled their garbage as building materials. But perhaps most impressive of all were the *puquios*: complex aqueduct systems that funnelled water from underground sources to reservoirs and fields. In this parched high desert plateau, water was more precious than gold. In order to survive they had to conserve every drop. That fact, more than anything else, may be the best clue we have as to their true purpose.

The first official study began just after the Second World War, when flights began passing overhead and the Lines were noticed for the first time. A German-born teacher, Maria Reiche, began formal surveys and is credited with their initial conservation. She believed the drawings matched constellations in the sky, but more recently this theory has been discredited. What is emerging now is a picture of the Lines as not mere representations, but pathways – enormous stages for religious ceremonies in which the entire community participated. In this view the Nazca Lines are more like a pilgrimage than a work of art, with rituals and offerings left at key intervals including rare shells and smashed pots.

But there may have been a practical purpose too. If water was survival then it is possible that the Lines were also a kind of map, marked down on the earth, to help future generations locate the precious sources of their *puquios*. Indeed there have been numerous overlaps discovered between where the drawings are found and where fresh underground sources of water are located. Trapezoids seem to point to an underground well; circles to a fountain; the beak of a hummingbird signals a river under the earth. The Lines could thus be seen to serve a dual purpose: to both locate and worship the most precious resource of the entire community – water.

There are fun theories too. Those imagining the Nazca as the world's first hot-air balloonists, floating above their works to admire them from the sky, and others that the Lines are a landing zone for alien beings. Whatever you believe, that the Lines hold meaning is undoubtedly true. This was a civilisation that thrived in one of the driest and most inhospitable places on Earth. They survived because they understood that water is life. Without it we would shrivel and die like the desert itself. It's wonderful to think of the mysteries that the Nazca Lines may hold. But their real message may well be simpler and more profound.

WHERE: Nazca Desert, Peru.

HOW TO SEE IT: For the best view, book an early morning flight from the town of Nazca.

TOP TIP: Take anti-nausea medication – it can be a bumpy ride.

TRY THIS INSTEAD: La Paracas Candelabra is an alternative prehistoric geoglyph in Peru's Ballestas Islands. The islands are also a world-class wildlife destination in their own right. www.peru.travel

SALAR DE UYUNI, BOLIVIA

The Salar de Uyuni is the world's largest salt flat. Covering roughly 4,000 square miles of south-western Bolivia, this enormous, stark white plane stretches out to an infinite horizon of dazzling hexagonal patterns carved in wind and grains of salt. It is more than 80 times larger than the Bonneville Salt Flats in Utah – made famous as the site of numerous land speed records since 1914. And it is the flattest place on the planet: in an area the size of the Big Island of Hawaii there is a variation in height of only 30 inches – and that is due solely to minute fluctuations in gravity because of the curvature of the Earth. There simply cannot be anywhere more level. As a

Photo: Entropy1963

result it is used by NASA to calibrate the altimeters on their satellites. Even Neil Armstrong noted it sparkling from space.

But what's truly spectacular about this vast salt pan, 12,000 feet up in a remote high plain of the Andes, is that it's also the largest natural mirror in the world. For most of the year the Salar is as dry as a desert, but in the rainy season, between November and March, a shallow film of water collects on the surface. The effect is mesmerising: the entire world is seen in reflection, earth and sky become indistinguishable. Come in the day and you will be walking on clouds, at night you will be floating in the Milky Way itself. Locals call it 'Heaven on Earth' because of the way it resembles the classic view of a celestial eternal paradise, and they may just be right.

The Salar de Uyuni was created 12,000 years ago when a vast inland sea, which once flooded this plain, dried up. A deep crust of salt, at places 30 feet thick, was all that remained. The local Aymara people have been harvesting this natural resource for generations: scraping piles from the ground to be dried and harvested into the condiment that's sprinkled around the world.

But the deserting water left something more valuable too. Buried under this crust of salt is a vast reservoir of briny water that is estimated to contain 9 million tonnes of lithium, more than a quarter of the world's known resources. And lithium is the new gold: used to power everything from the battery in your phone to the engine in electric cars. In our power-hungry economy, demand for lithium batteries is growing roughly 20 per cent every year. Salar de Uyuni could become one of the great clean energy reserves of the next century.

That's good news for the climate: the development of electric cars has been slowed by underpowered lithium batteries. A major new resource could kick start the industry and help provide a viable alternative to fossil fuels. It's good news for the people too. Many Bolivians are impoverished. The grandchildren of the peasants struggling to scrape salt today could reap huge rewards from a lithium harvest in the future. But the price will be high. Trenches, evaporation ponds and industry will fill the Salar. Extraction plants are already being built today. There are concerns of the effects of such mining downstream. To save the planet we may end up destroying heaven on Earth. See it now, before it's too late.

WHERE: Uyuni, Bolivia.

HOW TO SEE IT: The salt flats are only accessible by guided tour. Pick one up from the town of Uyuni nearby. www.bolivia.travel

TOP TIPS: Come January to March to see the Salar's incredible reflections. For a spectacular accommodation option it's possible to rent an Airstream trailer and stay overnight in the middle of the plain.

TRY THIS INSTEAD: The Bonneville Salt Flats are about an hour west of Salt Lake City. Come in the summer for the races. www.utah.com

RIO DE JANEIRO CARNIVAL, BRAZIL

The Rio de Janeiro Carnival in Brazil is the biggest party on the planet: five days of non-stop music, dancing and glittering costumes set around one of the most spectacular cities on Earth. Two million people a day take to the streets.

Hundreds of street parties fill the city. It dwarfs New Year's Eve in Times Square, deafens Glastonbury Festival in the UK and makes New Orleans's Mardi Gras look like a quiet get together among friends.

The carnival begins on the Friday before Ash Wednesday, 40 days before Easter, each year. Its roots can be traced back thousands of years, from ancient Greek spring festivals and Roman feasts to Catholic pre-Lent celebrations. More recently, in the 18th century, Rio hosted enormous water fights on the streets at this time, called the *Entrudo*, brought over from Portuguese immigrants, which evolved into increasingly elaborate parades. But those were mostly for society's elite. It wasn't until the second half of the 20th century that the carnival exploded into a party for the entire world.

The highlight of the five-day event is the samba parade. These infectious rhythms were introduced to Brazil by African slaves. They became the soundtrack of the working-class ghettos, the favelas, that surround the city. Although samba music has now spread across the country, and the world, at its core it is still the voice of the poor. And the Rio Carnival is their biggest stage.

Each favela has its own samba school, which competes for the honour of being crowned carnival champions. Thousands of performers are involved – from drummers and dancers to flag bearers and the scantily clad Carnival Queen. Their parade lasts less than 80 minutes, but the schools will work all year to prepare their routine. The shows are judged on a variety of criteria from the precision of the percussionists to the evolution of the choreography and the beauty of the costumes and floats.

And the pride of the entire community is at stake. People support their local samba school with the same passion they support their local football team. A successful school raises the self-esteem of the entire community – and helps to provide income and social support too. Just as importantly, for a few short minutes, these ordinary men and women are the stars of the biggest show on the planet. They help to transport their neighbourhoods away from their everyday lives and into something filled with spectacle and beauty.

That's why the Rio Carnival is a wonder of the world. Because celebrations, at their most fundamental, are about more than just having a good time. Music and dance are as important to human life as food and water. We've been letting loose since we could stamp our feet on the African savannah. Celebrations lift us out of the mundane and transport us to a world of transcendence and awe. They make us glad to be alive and life worth living. Celebrations shine a light on the best of who we are. And the Rio Carnival is the biggest spotlight of all.

WHERE: Rio de Janeiro, Brazil.

HOW TO SEE IT: To see the samba parade you need to buy tickets for the Sambadrome. The parade lasts two days, but the highlight is the parade of champions when the best twelve schools compete for the top prize. The best seats are in the middle and at the end of the runway, from sectors 6 to 11. www.visitbrasil.com

TOP TIPS: Go and see the top samba schools rehearsing for free in the run up to the carnival. The street band of Ipanema is the most famous and flamboyant street party. Numerous balls are held throughout the city too: Copacabana Palace Carnival Ball, Gay Gala and the Black Beads Party are some of the best. www.rio-carnival.net

Photo: Alexandre Macieira/Agência Brasil

TRY THIS INSTEAD: The Salvador Carnival is less famous and less structured than Rio, but if you like dancing in the streets it's arguably just as good. The carnival is free, but it's possible to buy a pass to dance in a designated safe area or to watch the show from a *camarote* – a small cabin with food and drink provided.

www.salvadorcarnival.info

EUROPE

THE ACROPOLIS, ATHENS

The Acropolis of Athens is the most important monument of ancient Greek civilisation. Looking over the city, from high on the sacred rock of Athens, this complex of ruined temples, statues and sanctuaries represents the pinnacle of Greek antiquity's culture and achievements. It is testimony to the ancient Greeks' advances in philosophy, politics, science and art and a symbol of the debts that our society still owes them today. The Acropolis of Athens is, arguably, the definitive monument of the Western world.

It has had many lives. Rising 490 feet above the city, the seven-acre site had superb natural defences and was used as a fortress as early as the 13th century BC. But by the 5th century BC it was beginning to take on a larger significance. Empowered, and enriched, by their recent revenge on the Persians for the sacking of Athens in 480 BC, the city began a lavish rebuilding programme. The people wanted the new

Acropolis to be a symbol of Athens. This was the centre of the Greek empire: the great rays of their influence radiated from this spot. The Acropolis was to be their shining example to the world. The site is composed of many buildings: the Erechtheion, the Propylaea and the Temple of Athena Nike. But the Parthenon is, undoubtedly, the most spectacular.

Under the direction of the great statesman Pericles, the first stone was laid on 28 July 447 BC. No expense was spared. The finest architects, sculptors and artisans were hired – including Phidias, considered the greatest artist of his day, who created the statue of Zeus at Olympia, one of the Seven Wonders of the Ancient World. But although the Parthenon is seen today as the epitome of Greek architecture, it was unlike anything that had come before it.

For starters, it was the first Greek temple to be built entirely of marble – 22,000 tonnes of it were hauled up on sledges and pulleys from quarries more than ten miles away. It was also the largest temple of its kind ever built, featuring an expanded base of eight 34-foot-high columns in front and seventeen on the side. This allowed an unprecedented amount of sculptural detail. Huge rectangular panels, called metopes, covered every inch of the façade, depicting battles of gods and Greek victories over their enemies. The two triangular pediments were filled with more than twenty larger-than-life marble figures. An enormous 525-foot sculpted frieze, portraying scenes of civic celebration – an expression of Athens' burgeoning democracy – circled the entirety of the temple's inner sanctum. And in the heart of it, most impressive of all, stood a 40-foot tall gold and ivory statue of Athena – patron goddess of the city and the Parthenon alike.

But even more remarkable was the way it was built. There are almost no straight lines in the entire building. The

base, and entablature above the columns, bend towards the middle; the steps curve upwards; the metopes tilt outward; each column bulges as if pressed down by the weight above. These subtle refinements, masterfully combined in proportion with one another, impart a sense of dynamism and vitality – as if the Parthenon is a living mass, flexing and straining under its great importance. How they built such a complicated work in less than fifteen years is a wonder in itself.

But its grandeur did not last long. Less than a decade after construction had finished, war broke out with Sparta and Greece suffered a humiliating defeat and a devastating plague. The Acropolis would remain standing for centuries, but its glory would never be the same. And then, in the early 19th century, another tragedy struck. Thomas Bruce, the Earl of Elgin – a Scottish aristocrat who was British ambassador to the Ottoman court – removed large parts of the frieze, most of the pediment statues and a number of the metopes in order to sell them to the British Museum, where they are still on display today. Whether he is viewed as a saviour (in his day locals would use parts of the Acropolis for building their own homes) or a criminal, and whether these works should be returned to Greece, is still a matter of bitter contention.

What is certain is that the Acropolis of Athens, and in particular the Parthenon, is the greatest standing testament to one of the most enlightened societies that ever lived. The ancient Greeks designed the concept of democracy. They built the foundation of Western philosophic thought and gave birth to some of the greatest, and still influential, thinkers the world has ever seen: Plato, Socrates, Aristotle. They brought us the origins of theatre and created the Olympic Games. They advanced art, mathematics and medicine. The world we live in today would be unrecognisable without the contribution of the ancient Greeks.

That's what makes the Acropolis of Athens special. All these strands come together here in one masterful creation. Pericles boasted: 'We shall be the marvel of the present day and of ages yet to come'. And he was right. The Acropolis is more than just a monument – it's the birthplace of all we hold dear and a reminder of the possibilities that we may still yet achieve.

WHERE: Athens, Greece.

HOW TO SEE IT: Open 8am to 8pm daily. Take the metro to the Acropolis station and walk up from there.
http://odysseus.culture.gr/index_en.html

TOP TIPS: Go late in the day. From 5pm the coach and cruise tours have all left, meaning you'll have the site, and sunset, all to yourself. The summer is very hot, try to avoid this time of year if possible. The Acropolis Museum nearby has excellent exhibitions of the Parthenon sculptures and more than 3,000 other artefacts from the region.
www.theacropolismuseum.gr/en

TRY THIS INSTEAD: The ancient Oracle of Delphi, at the foot of Mount Parnassos two hours west of Athens, is one of the most spectacular monuments in the entire country. Combine this with your trip to the Acropolis.
http://odysseus.culture.gr/index_en.html

STONEHENGE, ENGLAND

Stonehenge is one of the most important prehistoric monuments in the world. Built over the course of 1,500 years this 108-foot ring of concentric standing stones is one of the oldest man-made structures in the world. And yet, despite its antiquity, the sophistication of its architecture, and the challenges presented by its construction, are so enormous that its very existence has baffled people for centuries. How it was built, by whom and why is still shrouded in mystery. But recently some answers have started to emerge.

Stonehenge has been a sacred site for millennia. Located on Salisbury Plain in Wiltshire, England, the earliest archaeological records date back at least 10,000 years. At this time much of southern England was covered in woodland, but these chalky plains would have remained open, giving the site, it is thought, a special significance. Construction on Stonehenge itself began about 5,000 years ago and was eventually completed in three stages, by three separate groups of people.

First, around 3000 BC, a large earthwork barrow, or mound, was dug from the ground using tools made from antlers and then made into an inner and outer bank. Circling this 320-foot ring are the Aubrey Holes, 56 round pits about one metre across, which once contained timber posts or stones thought to be for burial and religious purposes.

The second, and most dramatic, stage of construction began in 2500 BC. Bluestones, which form the central ring of the henge and weigh roughly four tonnes each, were brought in from the Preseli Hills in Pembroke, South-west Wales, some 160 miles away. At that time, work on Stonehenge Avenue, a two-mile earthwork monument connecting the

River Avon to the north-east entrance of the henge, also began. Five hundred years later, in 2000 BC, the giant sarsen stones, which form the outer ring and the inner horseshoe-shaped trilithons, each one 30 feet tall and weighing as much as 30 tonnes, were transported from the Marlborough Downs, twenty miles to the north.

For many years it was thought impossible that a Stone Age people would have the engineering knowledge and tools to erect these enormous monoliths. But modern engineering simulations have presented a solution. Once on site, it is thought, holes were dug in the ground and one end of the stone was hauled over them, with great levers placed underneath, until gravity tipped it inside. Now, resting at 30°, a system of stone counterweights and teams of men, using plant-fibre ropes, would pull it vertical and the hole would then be filled to keep it in place. Finally, an earth ramp was piled up against the upright stones and the horizontal lintels were dragged into place. They were then fastened together vertically, using carved mortice and tenon joints, and horizontally, by tongue and groove joints. The complexity of these techniques, and the intricate shaping of stones that was required, has never been seen in any other prehistoric monuments from this time.

The final stage began in the heart of the Bronze Age, around 1500 BC, when the highly advanced Wessex people arrived and carved elaborate drawings of axe-heads and daggers into the stones and finalised their arrangement into what we see today. It is estimated that in total something in the region of 30 million man-hours went into the construction of Stonehenge, making it one of the greatest collaborative undertakings in human history.

But how did they get the stones there in the first place? It's a question that has perplexed scholars for centuries. Without

Photo: Archangel12

the wheel, or sophisticated tools, roughly 80 Pembroke bluestones, each one as heavy as an African elephant, had to be hauled for dozens of miles across rough and uneven ground. Legend has it that Merlin, under orders from King Arthur, used his magic to shrink the stones, which had originally been carried from Africa on the backs of giants, so that they could be transported to their present site. Other theories propose the movement of glaciers or even a race of ancient aliens as possible solutions – such is the enormity of the undertaking. The truth is less fantastical, but perhaps more remarkable for it.

Modern theories speculate that the smaller bluestones were most likely dragged on sledges and rollers to the headwaters of Milford Haven in Wales, loaded up on boats and sailed along the coast and up the River Avon to Somerset. Once there, they were unloaded and hauled again into their present position. The colossal weight of the giant sarsen stones from Wiltshire presented an even more complex problem. It would have taken 500 men to haul a single stone, and many more to get them up the steepest part of the route, at Redhorn Hill.

The question is why? What we know for sure is that the stones align perfectly with the midsummer sunrise and the midwinter sunset, suggesting they may have been used for astronomical purposes. At this time, great ceremonies would have been held too. Recent laser-scanning of the stones has shown that the outer edge of the north-east sarsens, which face the earthwork Avenue, were finely dressed and scraped clean, suggesting that this was the traditional processional entrance. At the time of solstice these carefully prepared stones would have glistened like stars in the sunlight.

It was also likely used as a sacred burial site of sorts. Funeral evidence has been found here that has been dated back thousands of years, to a time before even the stones were brought here. But there are fun theories about why Stonehenge was created too, including a druid temple, a stone-age calculator, a coronation site for Danish kings and a centre for healing. Whatever you believe, what is certain is that these stones have power. Their significance is palpable. To stand beside them is to stand in the footsteps of 5,000 years of worship, wonder and awe.

But as spectacular as it is, Stonehenge is only a small part of a much larger ancient landscape. There are more than 350 burial mounds and prehistoric monuments within the ten-square-mile World Heritage Site that surrounds it, including the Cursus, Woodhenge and Durrington Wall. Twenty-five miles north is the Avebury complex, the largest stone circle in the world, at nearly 1,500 feet across, and arguably the most impressive earthwork complex in Europe. Together these sites contain a vast source of knowledge about the ancient people of Great Britain and Europe, and are one of the most treasured archaeological sites in the world. But the magic of Stonehenge isn't about what it tells us. It's about how it feels. This ring of stones is a testament to the power of human will and collaboration. Walk beside them, watch the sunrise over them, look up at the stars and wonder who else may have once shared this view, and why.

WHERE: Near Amesbury, Wiltshire, England (just off the A303 road).

HOW TO SEE IT: English Heritage look after the property. It's open daily from 9.30am to 7pm, and there's a good visitor centre nearby with multiple exhibitions about the history of Stonehenge and the surrounding area.
www.english-heritage.org.uk

TOP TIP: Summer solstice is a huge party, with tens of thousands of visitors arriving to see the sunrise and sunset. If that's not your thing, come for the winter solstice instead. It's still possible to see the alignment of the stones, but with far fewer visitors.

TRY THIS INSTEAD: Avebury is an equally impressive prehistoric marvel, just 25 miles down the road. The stone circle here is actually much larger, though less sophisticated, and receives far fewer visitors. Pair this with your visit to Stonehenge.
www.english-heritage.org.uk

THE CHAUVET CAVE DRAWINGS, FRANCE

The Chauvet Cave in the Ardèche region of South-west France contains some of the greatest masterpieces of prehistoric art on the planet. The oldest known drawings, etched onto the cave walls with simple horse-hair brushes, charcoal and stones, were created by hunter-gatherers roughly 30,000 years ago – at a time when Europe was covered in 9,000 feet of glacier ice and giant aurochs still roamed the Earth. They are the oldest figurative cave drawings in Europe, and among the most ancient, sophisticated and well preserved in the world.

But they are more than just works of art. These drawings represent the birth of human creativity and imagination. They mark a turning point in our evolution. To see them is to look directly into the soul of our most primitive ancestors. And the more we look, the more we see ourselves reflected.

The Chauvet Cave was first discovered in 1994 by three amateur cavers, Jean-Marie Chauvet (who the cave was later named after), Éliette Brunel and Christian Hillaire. While exploring near the banks of the Ardèche River, they discovered an air current emanating from a small opening in a limestone cliff, a sign that there's an opening behind. They tunnelled their way into the darkness and what they found would soon stun the world.

Inside were over 1,000 individual drawings: mammoths, bison, owls, butterflies, a lion with red dots dripping from its snout like blood. There were skulls of now-extinct cave bears on the floor, the remnants of ancient hearths, a 25,000-year-old footprint of a small boy – now recognised to be the oldest human footprint ever recorded. Those three individuals were the first people to set foot in the cave for at least 20,000 years, yet the drawings they found were as fresh as the day they were first made.

In the months that followed, as anthropologists rushed in to study the find, it soon became apparent that the level of detail was unlike anything they'd encountered before. The artists of Chauvet had gone far beyond simple two-dimensional representations. They used the natural curvature of the cave to accentuate animal forms in three dimensions. They painted movement – ibex and reindeer running for their lives, rhinoceros horns crashing together in battle. We see multiple frames of a scene as if cut from a stop-motion film. There is shading and depth: the contrast of charcoal and stone. In flickering torchlight, as the artists themselves would have seen these drawings, the images appear to come alive.

But it is the emotion that they convey which is perhaps the most startling. On the 22-foot Panel of the Horses, one of the most celebrated drawings of the entire cave, we can

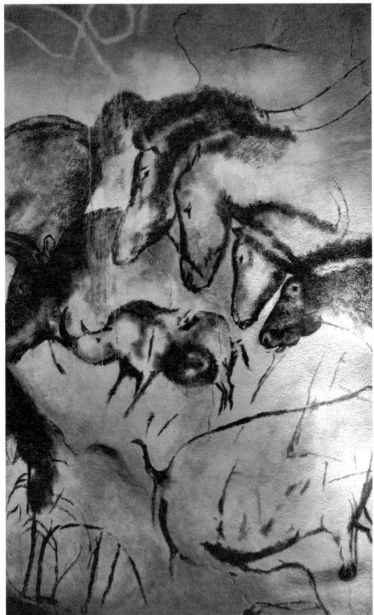

Photo: Thomas T.

look directly into the eyes of those animals and read their character as if they were standing next to us. On the Panel of Lions, we can feel the focus and ferocity of the lioness as she crouches mid-prowl. Using simple primitive tools they were able to create a tapestry of their prehistoric world that still breathes life today.

Similar caves often depict hunting scenes, but Chauvet is unique in its representation of large predators, many of which would have been rare to see. Typical of most cave art, there are no human figures. But in the last chamber, on a pinnacle of rock reaching down from the ceiling, there is a partial 'Venus' figure, the legs and genitals of a female, watched over by the 'Sorcerer', whose lower body is a man and upper body a bison. These facts together may offer a clue to the cave's purpose as a sacred site of ritual and ceremony, a kind of gateway to the spirit lands. The animals depicted were full of power and magic and would have aided these small tribes of humans as they navigated a dangerous and changing world.

When the drawings were finally dated there was another shock too: 30,000 years is nearly twice the age of all previous findings. It was the equivalent of finding a Picasso buried beneath the pyramids. According to all previous estimates, the Chauvet Cave simply should not have been possible. Since then other discoveries have been made, including a 40,000-year-old fragment of a pig-deer sketch found in the Sulawesi cave of Indonesia. As a result, we have had to revise our thinking about the development of art and creativity in mankind.

This was a time when *Homo sapiens* still shared the Earth with Neanderthals. While they were churning out crude rings and awls, our human ancestors were playing around with perspective and anatomical precision. This artistic ability may have coincided with a larger evolutionary leap. The birth of the artistic impulse, as witnessed in Chauvet, may have also heralded an expansion of our intellect and imagination. These drawings may be among the first truly human creations on Earth.

And that's why they're so powerful. The Chauvet paintings are a bridge through the aeons of history. To see them is to touch the memory of another soul and catch a glimpse, perhaps, of the genetic memory of us all. That there is significance to them, there is no doubt. But perhaps there need not be a practical purpose. Perhaps they were created, like all art is, in the end, for its own sake. Because there is a deep drive within us to mark our existence, to hold on somehow to all that we have seen and loved and feared and admired. Art makes us human. And it began here in the Chauvet Cave.

WHERE: Ardèche, France.

HOW TO SEE IT: In order to protect the Chauvet Cave it is not open to the public. Previous cave drawings, such as the painting in the Lascaux Cave nearby, have been irrevocably damaged through human contact. Instead, visit the new Chauvet museum, the Caverne du Pont D'Arc, a spectacular three-dimensional re-creation of the entire cave, painstakingly put together by teams of specialist artists. http://en.cavernedupontdarc.fr

TOP TIP: For a detailed look at the original cave drawings, watch award-winning documentary-maker Werner Herzog's beautiful and thought-provoking film *Cave of Forgotten Dreams.*

TRY THIS INSTEAD: The Altamira Cave in northern Spain has some of the oldest and most beautiful cave paintings in the world. And it's still possible to see them first hand, but it won't be easy. On a randomly selected day of the week, visitors to the Museo de Altamira nearby will be invited to enter a draw in which just five lucky people will be granted a short guided tour.
http://museodealtamira.mcu.es

LAKE BAIKAL, RUSSIA

Lake Baikal is the largest, oldest and deepest freshwater lake in the world. Located in south-eastern Siberia in Russia, and surrounded by jagged snow-shouldered mountains, taiga forests and vast frozen tundra on all sides, this enormous body of water is as breathtaking as it is astounding. At nearly 400 miles long, 50 miles wide and 1,300 miles around it may not be the largest lake by surface area (that honour falls to the Caspian Sea), but with its enormous depth of up to 5,000 feet, deeper than three Empire State Buildings stacked on top of one another, it is the largest volume of water by far. Beneath its surface lies a staggering 5,662 cubic miles of fresh water, 20 per cent of the world's unfrozen source – more than all of the Great Lakes of America combined. If it were emptied and Victoria Falls, the largest waterfall on the planet, were to pour into it continuously, 24 hours a day, it would take centuries to fill it up.

And every drop is pure. Low mineral content and tiny, filter-feeding shrimps known as *Epischura*, which keep it clean, have created some of the clearest water in the world. From the surface it's possible to see an object 130 feet below the water line. Jump in and you can drink while you swim. It is known as the 'Pearl of Siberia' and that's exactly what it resembles, an enormous turquoise jewel embedded deep in the Earth. During storms it rages like an ocean; calm, it reflects the vastness of the Russian sky as far as the eye can see.

It began forming about 25 million years ago, filling in a deep rift created by the movement of tectonic plates. In the future, as that movement continues, it will eventually tear apart and transform Baikal into a new sea. This antiquity has granted it a unique ecosystem. Of the more than 2,000 species of plant and animal found here, two-thirds exist nowhere else on Earth. The most unusual is the Nerpa, or Baikal seal, the only freshwater seal in the world, which can swim for more than an hour without a breath, descend to nearly 1,000 feet and give birth to their young on snow dens built up on the lake ice. But no one knows quite how they got here. Baikal is landlocked on all sides and their nearest cousin lives 2,000 miles away in the Arctic.

The people who make their home here are Russian Siberian and indigenous Buryats. Theirs is a community based on reverence for nature. For them, Lake Baikal is holy, known as the 'Sacred Sea'. In summer, air temperatures rise to 11°C, the heat retention from the water keeping surrounding temperatures mild. In winter, the thermometer plummets to –21°C, balmy compared with the –90°C regularly recorded elsewhere in Siberia. But the lake still freezes; water turns to ice six feet thick. During the Russo-Japanese war of 1904–5 the ice was so dense they were able to lay train tracks across the lake to transport supplies to the front.

Baikal holds many mysteries too. First, there are the circles. Astronauts regularly report the sudden appearance of perfect circular marks on the surface of the frozen lake.

Photo: Aleksandr Zykov

But despite popular claims to the contrary, it's not extra-terrestrial activity. Methane rises from the lakebed, creating a rising funnel of warmer water, which swirls in a circular pattern, marking the surface of the ice from underneath. But that doesn't mean there are no aliens at all. This is one of the world's biggest UFO hotspots; sightings are reported all the time. Most intriguing of all is a series of recently declassified Soviet documents that reveal a plane crashed in the lake in 1958, after the pilots were reportedly pursued by a strange craft. And even better was an event in 1982 when a team of Russian Navy divers encountered a group of humanoid creatures in silvery suits, 150 feet below the surface. After trying to pursue them, three divers were killed and four were seriously injured. The 'creatures', or whatever they were, were never identified.

And that's not all. In 1977, a deep-water submersible called *Paysis* was conducting scientific research, in complete darkness at a depth of 4,000 feet, when a sudden bright spotlight shone on them for several seconds from an unknown source. It has never been explained.

And then there are the disappearances. Locals tell of various places in the lake where ships simply disappear, never to be seen again. The most famous example happened on 16 June 2011, when a crew of experienced sailors on board the 'Yamaha' set off from a village in the Kabansk area of Buryatia. A sudden fog rolled in, their instruments failed and when the fog rolled back they were simply gone. To this day no wreckage has ever been found and no one knows what happened. It might have been that an enormous whirlpool suddenly formed and sucked them to the bottom. Buryat legends speak of chasms in the water, which are gateways to hell. Then again, it might have been the monster. Native people call it 'Lusud-Khan' or 'Usan-Lobson Khan', Water

Dragon Master. Accounts go back thousands of years, from cave painting to notes in travellers' books. Or maybe that was just one of the infamous Baikal visions. Fishermen here regularly report seeing anything from trains and old ships to castles and alien vessels floating above the lake. These, at least, however, are not supernatural. The atmospheric conditions here have created layers of different temperature air, which refracts light in unusual ways. Objects on distant shores are literally lifted, as if they were a hologram, and placed hovering on the lake's surface, like ghosts.

The biggest, the oldest, the deepest and also, quite possibly, the most mysterious and bizarre, Lake Baikal is an awe-inspiring place now … but who knows what new wonders, supernatural or not, may one day be revealed beneath its icy surface?

WHERE: Siberia, Russia.

HOW TO SEE IT: Lake Baikal is in an extremely remote location, but there are a few options for tourists. The most popular base is the village of Listvyanka, two hours' drive from the city of Irkutsk, which has flights from many domestic cities and a few international destinations. Olkhon is also a popular base, the largest of Baikal's 45 islands. July and August are the best months to travel or, if you're feeling brave, try March for winter activities.
www.lakebaikal.org

TOP TIP: Combine a visit to Lake Baikal with a trip on the Trans-Siberian Railway, one of the world's great train journeys, covering a staggering 6,600 miles and eight time zones from Moscow to Vladivostok. Most itineraries take about two weeks and include a day's stop at Lake Baikal.

TRY THIS INSTEAD: America's Great Lakes may not be quite as big, but they are just as stunning. Combine Lake Ontario with Niagara Falls, Lake Michigan with Chicago, Lake Superior with Voyageurs National Park and Lake Huron with Canada's Georgian Bay.

www.greatlakesusa.co.uk

THE COLOSSEUM, ROME

The ancient Roman empire once spread across three continents from Hadrian's Wall in northern England to the Euphrates in Syria; the River Rhine to the Black Sea. It lasted for more than 1,000 years in the West and more than 2,000 in the east. It founded London, Cologne and hundreds of other towns and cities. Its army, the feared Roman Legion, controlled nearly half of the known world. In the course of human history there have been few empires that match the greatness of Rome.

But the Empire didn't govern by brute force alone. People aspired to be Roman. The Romans brought wealth, education and security. They expanded on Greek architecture, philosophy and science. Their political and justice systems still serve as inspiration for our institutions today. The Romans have left many monuments: from roads and aqueducts to temples, bridges and beautiful works of art. But of all that remains, there is perhaps no better symbol of their great empire than the Colosseum.

Construction of the Colosseum began in AD 72 by the emperor Vespasian, of the Flavian dynasty, and was finished in AD 80 by his son Titus, who celebrated its opening with 100 days of games. At the time, it was the largest amphitheatre that had ever been built. And the most spectacular too. Standing more than 150 feet tall and 600 feet long, with seating for 50,000 people, its four stories, three with enormous superimposed arches, were designed to impress. In its prime it was covered in marble; the ceilings were painted stuccos, the exterior was adorned with glistening bronze shields and the main entrance was marked by giant porticoes, each topped by a gilded horse-drawn chariot. This was the ultimate symbol of Roman power and prosperity.

But its beauty belied its bloody purpose. The Colosseum was built to win favour with the people of Rome. It was, by and large, a propaganda tool, used to simultaneously entertain and intimidate. All were able to attend, from dignitaries down to the lowliest citizen. And all wanted death. Inside the arena, gladiators, usually slaves, prisoners of war or condemned criminals, would wage savage battles, pitting different fighting styles and weapons from the far reaches of the empire against one another. And no quarter was given. Unless spared by the emperor himself, there could be only one survivor. The arena's sandy floor was dyed red to hide the stains of blood.

Combat with animals was popular too. Exotic beasts were brought back to Rome from across the empire to fight. Beneath the arena there were 32 cages, containing an array of deadly animals, which could be hauled up on elevators by slaves and then let loose onto the stage. The *bestiarius*, a gladiator who specialised in duelling these wild beasts, was one of the most revered of all fighters, but could expect a short career, even by gladiatorial standards.

But successful gladiators were the rock stars of the day. They drew thousands of fans, enjoyed lavish gifts and

Photo: Diana Ringo

could even be awarded freedom if they'd tallied up enough kills. Some are still remembered: Flamma, a Syrian slave, who fought 34 times and refused the *rudis*, the offer of his freedom, four times before finally succumbing in the ring; Carpophores, who famously defeated a bear, a lion and a leopard in a single battle; Priscus and Verus, two legendary rivals who fought viciously for hours without a victor, before simultaneously laying down their swords in respect.

At times famous battles were re-enacted too, with casts of hundreds of slaves and prisoners slaughtered before the baying crowd. The lower level could even be flooded, a marvel of engineering at the time, in order to stage naval battles. In one famous encounter Titus brought in 3,000 men and dozens of ships to wage ocean war against each other on an artificial sea.

But however bloody its history, we should remember the Colosseum not just for its savageness, but for its glory too. The Romans gave us the alphabet, they invented trial by jury. Their language is the foundation of most European tongues. Their art and engineering continue to inspire. The Romans shaped our world beyond recognition and the Colosseum was their greatest work.

WHERE: Piazza del Colosseo, Rome, Italy.

HOW TO SEE IT: Take Metro Line B to the 'Colosseo'. Open from 8.30am to 4.30pm in winter and to 7.15pm in summer. www.coopculture.it/the-colosseum.cfm

TOP TIPS: Avoid the queues by arriving early (before 8.30am), booking an official guided tour (which skips the line) or purchasing your ticket in advance from the Palatine Hill entrance nearby. The first Sunday of the month is free.

TRY THIS INSTEAD: The Pantheon, also in Rome, is a beautifully preserved temple and one of the greatest architectural marvels from the Roman era. Combine with the Colosseum for a perfect day in Rome.
www.pantheonroma.com

SAGRADA FAMÍLIA, SPAIN

Gaudí's masterpiece cathedral, the Sagrada Família in Barcelona, is a work of staggering architectural genius. But it's absolutely absurd too. Buttercup-shaped ceilings glow in spores of purple, blue and yellow. Columns twist like plant stems. There are honeycomb caverns and pinnacles that look like blades of quartz grass. At first glance it's as if a child's doodle has been grotesquely brought to life. But then there is the familiarity: instead of gargoyles, amphibians slither down the sides of his church, instead of straight lines the world twists like trees. That is Gaudí's genius: order has been replaced by nature. 'The Great Book' as he called it, the Earth itself, is his inspiration. Walking into the Sagrada Família is like entering a forest of dreams.

And that's exactly what he intended. 'Originality is returning to the origin', he would often say. That origin was nature. Gaudí was an extremely religious man. Nature, for him, was God's perfect creation. The natural world was a representation of God Himself. By honouring the Earth, his cathedral would honour God in a new, and more fitting, way.

And he didn't hold back. Towers rise like ears of corn from the top of the temple, stairs spiral like seashells. Everywhere curves and flows; the straight lines of mankind have been banished. There is colour too. Bright ceramics detail the façades like lizard skin. Stained-glass windows illuminate the walls. The sun's rays pour through the ceiling like dappled leaves. Look up and it is as if you are standing beneath the canopy of an enormous forest.

But Gaudí did not merely copy nature. He analysed its structural components and then applied those principles to his designs. He understood that nature inherently creates in the strongest, lightest and most efficient ways. He didn't just want his church to look like a forest, he wanted it to be built like a forest. Columns resemble tree trunks, but they also support the ceiling of the church in exactly the same way a tree's branches support its crown. Roofs mirror the shape of leaves in order to make them lighter and better able to channel rainwater. Arches droop like inverted wet reeds, making them stronger than traditional semi-circular designs. Nature has been perfecting its construction for millions of years, all we need do, Gaudí teaches us, is to observe, admire and learn.

It's an idea that's rapidly catching on. Today, advances in digital technology and 3D printing are expanding the scope of Gaudí's vision exponentially and architects around the world are increasingly turning to the natural world for their inspiration. Termite mounds are being studied to see how we can ventilate buildings with minimal energy. The Japanese bullet train was inspired by a Kingfisher beak. Germany's revolutionary BIQ building incorporates living algae into its transparent shell, naturally regulating the amount of light and shade let into the building.

And it's not just architecture. Biomimicry, as it is known, is infiltrating all aspects of our life. The iridescence in butterfly wings has led to brighter mobile phone screens and anti-counterfeiting technology. The eyes of a 45-million-year-old fly trapped in amber have inspired a new design of solar panel. The serrated proboscis of a mosquito, which minimises nerve stimulation, is being copied in the design of hypodermic needles to reduce the pain of injections. Raptors are changing the way airplane wings are built. Tropical birds are inspiring cosmetics. And we haven't even scratched the surface. Spider silk is five times stronger by weight than steel. Glow-worms produce a light with almost no energy loss. There is a beetle that can detect the infrared radiation of a forest fire more than 50 miles away. Nature-inspired technology may well be the industrial revolution of our generation. And it began here, with Gaudí's masterpiece, the Sagrada Família.

But he never saw it completed. Gaudí began work on it in 1883 and spent the next 47 years of his life consumed by the project, until his death in 1926. But the project is so vast and complicated that it is not expected to be finished until at least 2026 – 100 years after his death. There is something profoundly moving about that. Not just because it's so rare, in our modern lives, to see something conceived and realised over multiple generations. But also because we are here, now, at the birth of it. So much of what we celebrate as wondrous is inherited from antiquity. But this is a wonder for our time, and for the future too. And that's exactly how Gaudí intended it. He saw the Sagrada Família as the first in a new era of religious buildings – one that fitted our post-industrial, secularised world. Instead of the imposing churches of the past, Gaudí built a forest. Instead of riches, he gave us flowers. Gaudí reminds us that all we need to do to connect with our spirit, with something greater than ourselves, is return to our origin. Return to the Earth itself.

WHERE: Barcelona, Spain.

Photo: Sagrada Família (official)

HOW TO SEE IT: Open 9am to 6pm in winter, to 8pm in summer. The L5 (blue) and L2 (purple) metro lines have stops across the street.
www.sagradafamilia.org/en

TOP TIPS: The lines to get inside can be very long, so buy your tickets in advance online. It's possible to climb up into the towers, but beware: if you're scared of heights, or claustrophobic, don't go. The Passion Towers give you a better view of the ocean. The Nativity Towers give you better views of the mountains.

TRY THIS INSTEAD: Barcelona is filled with Gaudí's work, including Parc Güell, Casa Batlló and many more homes, buildings, parks and attractions.
www.barcelonaturisme.com

THE LARGE HADRON COLLIDER, SWITZERLAND

The Large Hadron Collider (LHC) is the biggest and most complicated machine ever built. Located more than 300 feet underground at the CERN facility in Geneva, this 17-mile tunnel is designed to accelerate and then smash together sub-atomic particles, the building blocks of the universe. The resulting energy splits those particles into even smaller pieces. But it also recreates the conditions immediately after the Big Bang. The LHC is like a time machine that transports us back 14 billion years to the birth of the universe itself. But it's transporting us forward too. This is a machine that, by all rights, should be pure science fiction. But it's not. And it's fundamentally changing our understanding of who we are and where we come from.

Building it wasn't easy. From initial conception to finished machine took more than 100,000 person-years of work – roughly the equivalent amount of time it took to build the Great Pyramid of Giza. The tunnel, which they use to accelerate the beams of particles, was adapted from a previous experiment. But enormous caverns had to be dug around it to house the four main detectors, the parts of the machine that record the results of the LHC's major experiments. Each detector is the biggest and most sophisticated of its kind ever built – some reaching the size of a twelve-storey block of flats.

The information these detectors collect is simply staggering, with roughly 30 petabytes of data produced annually. To put that in perspective: just one petabyte is the equivalent of 500 billion pages of standard printed text, which means the physicists at the LHC have 15 trillion pages of text to sift through each year. If one person were to read a single page of that data every minute, and never stop, it would take almost 3 million years for them to finish. Which is, obviously, impossible. So to process those enormous figures, the largest distributed computer grid ever conceived was built – a network of hundreds of thousands of processing cores, in more than 40 countries, working around the clock.

But it's what is inside the LHC that really blows your mind. To generate the necessary levels of energy, they must accelerate a beam of particles to 99.999999 per cent the speed of light. In a single second, that beam will travel around the seventeen-mile track 11,245 times. In ten hours, the average operating time of a single session, it would have travelled the equivalent of a trip to Neptune and back. Such enormous speeds can only be created in an ultra-high vacuum. To do

Photo: Maximilien Brice, CERN

that, they have to cool the chamber to −271.3°C, making the LHC the coldest place in our entire solar system, about one degree frostier than outer space itself.

Once inside the tube, two parallel particle beams containing either protons or lead ions, depending on the experiment, are hurtled in opposite directions. When they reach full velocity the beams are crashed together at specially designated junctions where the enormous detectors are placed. The energy produced is astronomical. At the point of impact the explosion is 100,000 times hotter than the centre of the sun. But the explosion is also infinitesimally small: the detectors have to precisely measure the location of each collision to within a few millionths of a metre. But they don't have much time. In order to pick up the exchange of post-collision particles, they have to record the passage of time to within a few billionths of a second. And that's just one collision. For every smash there are an estimated 600 million collisions per second.

Steering the beams isn't easy either. More than 1,700 superconducting electromagnets are used, averaging 50 feet tall and 30 tonnes each. But the largest in the entire project is over 2,000 tonnes – or the size of five jumbo jets, the biggest in the world. Feeding these magnets is an enormous network of superconducting cables so big that if you added all their filaments together they would stretch to the sun and back five times, with enough left over for a few trips to the moon.

But these are just statistics. The true wonder is why they're doing it in the first place. At present, 10,000 people use the LHC for research – more than half the world's theoretical physicists. They are involved with everything from studying the biological effects of antiprotons and how different fundamental particles interact to uncovering the secrets of anti-matter, dark matter and more. The most famous discovery of the LHC is, of course, the Higgs Boson, the 'God Particle', one of the primary reasons for the LHC's existence. The Higgs field, as it is known, is a kind of sub-atomic syrup through which all particles must pass. And by doing so, the field gives those particles mass. In a very real way, the Higgs transforms the invisible sub-atomic world into the world we see around us every day. Proving its existence was, undoubtedly, one of the most significant breakthroughs in scientific history, helping to confirm the Standard Model of physics, a theory that seeks to explain the goings on of the universe at a sub-atomic level. It may well also lead to the Holy Grail of physics – a unified theory of everything from the sub-atomic world of quantum mechanics to the general relativity of Einstein.

But its discovery poses more questions too. At the time of writing, a potential paradigm-shattering discovery had just been cautiously announced at the LHC, but had not yet been verified. The current understanding of the universe suggests that the four-dimensional world we live in (the three dimensions of space and the fourth dimension of time) is but a fraction of what is really out there. The universe is in fact composed of ten, and maybe more, dimensions that we cannot perceive. But the pure mathematics of theoretical physics thinks that they're there. And the LHC may have proved it.

A mere blink ago in the lifespan of the Earth, human beings sparked a fire with two rocks and used the bones of animals to make clubs. Now we are building machines that can give us a glimpse of the origins of the universe itself. But the LHC is more than just the most sophisticated tool ever built. It's a gateway to the future: to our future understanding of ourselves and the universe to which we are inextricably bound.

WHERE: CERN Facility, Geneva, Switzerland.

HOW TO SEE IT: Regular guided tours are available of the CERN facility. And if you can't make it, virtual tours are also available online.
http://visits.web.cern.ch/tours/guided-tours

TOP TIP: Watch the award-winning documentary *Particle Fever* for an insight into how the LHC was built and operates.

TRY THIS INSTEAD: Fermi National Accelerator Laboratory, 35 miles west of Chicago, is America's premier particle physics laboratory and offers regular guided tours, lectures and other events.
www.fnal.gov

MIDDLE EAST

OLD CITY JERUSALEM, ISRAEL

The Old City of Jerusalem is the spiritual heart of the three major monotheistic religions: Judaism, Christianity and Islam. Measuring less than half of a square mile, it nonetheless contains more than 200 monuments, including some of the most treasured and fought over land on Earth. Half the world's population believe this to be the most sacred place on the planet. But its holy purpose belies its violent history; and that bitter contention is still being fought on its streets today. The Old City of Jerusalem represents our highest ideals, but also our most divisive and dogmatic depths. It is, perhaps, in all its glory and bloodied past, the definitive monument to the human soul.

It's also one of the oldest continuously inhabited places on Earth, with a history that stretches back more than 5,000 years. Inside the Old City is a labyrinth of narrow passageways, markets and stone towers surrounded by a 16th-century defensive wall. There are four districts: the Muslim quarter, the Jewish quarter, the Christian quarter and the Armenian quarter, each one containing a treasure trove of religious shrines that reflect the spiritual heritage of each unique culture.

But the Old City is not just a cold archaeological site. More than 30,000 people still live here: Christians, Muslims and Jews, side by side. The sound of their worship fills the air day and night. Perhaps more so than anywhere else on Earth, history feels alive here, still flexing and pulsing with the religious fervour that carved, and is still shaping, this hallowed ground. To walk these streets is a wonder in itself. But there are a number of monuments that stand out.

In the Christian quarter, the Church of the Holy Sepulchre is without a doubt the most important. It was here that Jesus Christ was crucified, following his final walk along the Via Dolorosa, or the Stations of the Cross. Many Christians also believe this to be the location of his tomb and subsequent resurrection from the dead.

In the Jewish quarter it is the Western Wall, or Wailing Wall, built by King Herod in 20 BC. This was originally the site of the Second Temple, one of Judaism's most important places of worship, until it was destroyed by the Romans in AD 70. All that remained was this 62-foot stone wall and it has been revered as a holy place ever since.

Nearby is the Temple of the Mount, the most fought-over

Photo: Guggianij

piece of land in the history of human civilisation. For Jews this is the place where God gathered the dust to create Adam and Abraham nearly sacrificed his son to prove his faith. It is here also that the First Temple of the Jews was built by King Solomon in the 10th century BC, before it was torn down 400 years later by the Babylonian king Nebuchadnezzar.

But the Temple of the Mount is also shared with the Muslim quarter. Here it is called Haram al-Sharif, the Noble Sanctuary. It houses the Dome of the Rock, a 7th-century timber-framed shrine and masterpiece of Islamic architecture encasing the rock from which the Prophet Muhammad is said to have ascended to heaven. The Dome of the Rock is also the oldest extant Islamic monument in the world and the basis for almost all Islamic architecture and art since.

And therein lies the problem. The Temple of the Mount is claimed by both ideologies. Both hold it sacred, and both are right. Today, Israel has political sovereignty over the territory that surrounds the Temple Mount, but the compound itself is managed by an Islamic organisation called the Waqf. Israel sees their presence here as a reunification of their ancient capital; Palestinians deem them to be occupiers in Arab land (a position also held by the United Nations). And their conflict is not new. Religious wars have been waged over these precious monuments of the Old City, an area less than a third of the size of Central Park in New York, for thousands of years. And, as far as anyone can tell, there is no end in sight.

But that's also what makes the Old City of Jerusalem so important. Some wonders fill us with awe, some with humility, admiration and respect. But some should also make us think. If the Old City of Jerusalem is the definitive monument of the human soul, then it is perhaps here that we must begin to reconcile it too. This tiny patch of Earth may have become a reminder of what divides us, but it is also a beacon of all that we share and all that may unite us still.

WHERE: Jerusalem, Israel.

HOW TO SEE IT: May and October can often be the quietest months, with mild temperatures. Come during religious holidays for a special atmosphere.
www.goisrael.com

TOP TIPS: Visit Monday to Thursday. Friday is the Muslim day of prayers, Saturday is the Jewish Sabbath and Sunday is the Christian day of rest – religious sites will either be closed or with restricted access. Be aware of the dress codes at religious sites before you travel.

TRY THIS INSTEAD: In Jewish, Islamic and Christian history, Mount Sinai in Egypt is believed to be the site where Moses received the Ten Commandments. Thousands of pilgrims make the trek to the summit each year.
www.egypt.travel

BURJ KHALIFA, UNITED ARAB EMIRATES

The Burj Khalifa is the tallest building in the world. Soaring 2,716 feet over Dubai in the United Arab Emirates, it is three times the height of the Eiffel Tower in Paris, and nearly twice the height of the Empire State Building in New York City. It can be seen from 60 miles away. If you laid all its pieces end to end, they would stretch a quarter of the way around the

Photo: Donaldytong

planet. In fact, it's so incredibly tall that it's possible to watch the sunset twice in a single day, once from the lower floors and then again from the top.

But the Burj Khalifa is more than just an impressive building. Skyscrapers are the cathedrals of our time. They represent the pinnacle of the industrial, modern and now technological revolution. They are the ultimate expression of human ambition and our mastery over the environment. There have been many impressive skyscrapers over the last century – the Petronas Twin Towers in Kuala Lumpur, the Willis Tower in Chicago – but the Burj Khalifa is the greatest ever built.

It has broken many world records. Aside from being the tallest building on the planet, it also holds the record for the tallest freestanding structure, most number of floors (160), highest occupied floor (level 153), highest outdoor observation deck (level 148, 1,823 feet), highest service elevator, longest distance travelled by an elevator (140 floors, travelling roughly ten metres per second), the highest restaurant (1,450 feet), highest nightclub (143rd floor) and highest place of worship (a mosque on the 158th floor). In total it took more than 110,000 tonnes of concrete, 55,000 tonnes of steel, 22 million man-hours, US$1.5 billion and six years to complete. It now comprises 1.85 million square feet of office and residential space – making it also one of the largest floor plans of a single building in the world.

Its architecture embodies a mixture of Islamic and contemporary influences. The design is based on a Spider Lily, a flower widely cultivated in Dubai and representative of Islamic art. But there is a distinctly futuristic feel about it too, with sleek chromatic lines tapering upwards in ever-decreasing steps. The entire building appears to spiral towards the sky, as if it is pulling upwards at its roots.

The spiral also has its origin in Islamic art's emphasis on geometric designs. In this way the Burj Khalifa can be seen as a kind of contemporary minaret: a bridge between East and West, blending the city's heritage with its ambitions on the world stage.

There are some clever technical components too. The Burj's Y-shaped plan allows for the greatest amount of window space without creating unusable internal areas. In order to ventilate the building it sucks air in from the top, where the temperature is significantly cooler and less humid. It has one of the largest condensation recovery systems in the world, 15 million gallons are collected sustainably every year. And in order to support its great height, a new type of structural core had to be developed, which employs three wings, each one supported by the two others. This design also allowed for more internal light and better wind resistance.

Burj Khalifa is a marvel of engineering and has redefined what is possible in the design and construction of super-tall buildings. But it holds a dark secret too: 12,000 workers a day were employed in its construction, many of them from poor neighbouring regions. There have been numerous reports alleging rampant exploitation of Dubai workers over the last few decades, many of whom are forced to work in unsafe conditions for very little pay. There is a tragic irony about this. The Burj Khalifa is one of the greatest symbols of 21st-century wealth and success, but if the allegations are proved correct, it was built on the foundation of cheap labour. There's a truth in that too. For all our glittering ambition, for all the modern towers and castles we build, we are still unable to provide basic needs for more than half the world. Perhaps, in the end, the Burj Khalifa will be remembered not just as a marvel of modern times, but also as a monument to its hidden costs. Here we see the startlingly rich and the starving poor, side by side. Our great achievements written in the ink of our great neglect.

WHERE: Dubai, United Arab Emirates.

HOW TO SEE IT: Tickets can be purchased for the observatory, restaurant and more online at: www.burjkhalifa.ae

TOP TIPS: Booking in advance is roughly four times cheaper than buying a ticket on the day. Sunset is the best time, but really popular too – book as far in advance as possible and make sure to try to catch the sunset twice, once from the bottom floors and again from the top.

TRY THIS INSTEAD: At 1,450 feet, the Willis Tower in Chicago is the tallest building in the western hemisphere. But what makes it truly unique is The Ledge: walk-in glass boxes with see-through floors that extend four feet out from the edge of the building's 103rd floor, making it just about possible to walk on air.
www.theskydeck.com

PETRA, JORDAN

The ancient rock-carved citadel of Petra in South-west Jordan is one of the most visually mind-blowing archaeological sites in the world. This prehistoric warren of temples and tombs has been hewn directly into the sandstone cliffs of a remote desert canyon. It is one of the most dramatic cities that has ever been built, and one of the most improbable too. Despite receiving only six inches of rain a year, the people who lived here thrived, sculpting masterpieces into the swirling red rock mountains and surrounding them with an oasis of orchards, gardens and pools. Petra, the Rose City as it's known, is one of the greatest wonders of the ancient world.

It was built in the 3rd century BC by the Nabataeans, a formerly nomadic tribe of Bedouins who rose to prominence through their skilful control of trading routes. Petra was located at the crossroads of two vital caravan routes, one connecting Syria and the Red Sea, the other linking the incense, silks and spices of the Far East with the Greek and Roman empires of the Mediterranean. The Nabataeans began by raiding these wealthy traders, but then later evolved to offering protection for safe passage instead. At a price. Within a few decades they had amassed enormous sums of wealth and a mercantile empire that stretched for hundreds of miles, from modern-day Israel into the northern Arabian Peninsula. Petra became their capital city.

But it was lost for centuries. After it was abandoned at the end of the 7th century, it remained hidden in the desert, a secret known only to the local Bedouin tribes, for more than 1,000 years. It wasn't until 1812, when a young Swiss adventurer named Johann Burckhardt posed as a local Bedouin and tricked his way into the vast rock citadel. He was the first outsider to set eyes on it in 600 years and the first Westerner to enter its gates since the Crusades.

What he saw stunned him then, as it still fills visitors with wonder to this day. Petra is entered via the *siq*, a three-quarter-mile winding, narrow canyon, in places no more than fifteen feet across, pressed in on either side by 200-foot cliff walls. Suddenly, in a clearing at the end of this gorge, the massive carved façade of al-Khazneh, The Treasury, comes into view. This giant tomb stands 120 feet tall, with ornate

Photo: Dennis Jarvis

columns, statues and decorated friezes sculpted directly into the mountain face. Further down the canyon, cut into the orange and ochre mountainsides, there is an enormous Roman amphitheatre and more than 800 finely carved tombs and temples. Near the end of the city, at the top of more than 800 rock steps, The Monastery, al-Deir, appears like the entrance to a mythical kingdom. At 120 feet high and 150 feet wide, this is the biggest monument in Petra: vast columns rise up to carved window recesses, sculpted pinnacles and an enormous urn on its crown. Nowhere is Petra's power and grace better balanced: the elegance of a palace cut straight into the side of a sheer cliff. And that's what makes this ancient city so special. The delicacy of the carvings blend into the immensity of the mountains with such harmony it is as if the desert itself is naturally morphing into perfect aesthetic forms.

But Petra is special for other reasons too. Despite being located in one of the driest places on Earth, the Nabataeans somehow turned this sandstone citadel into a fertile garden. Historians estimate that they managed to harness the winter rains and natural desert springs to such an extent that they were able to carry 12 million gallons of fresh water into the city each day, via a complicated series of cisterns, pools and covered waterways. This abundant water meant Petra's 20,000 inhabitants could not just bathe and drink to their heart's content, they could grow fruit and olive trees, vineyards and vast agricultural fields.

But, in many ways, such ingenuity is to be expected. Although the Nabataeans began as desert nomads, within a few centuries they had grown to become one of the most advanced civilisations of the ancient world, highly literate with sophisticated art and progressive values towards slaves and women. And many of their secrets are yet to be uncovered. Archaeologists estimate that 85 per cent of Petra is still buried under the desert sands. Burckhardt may have discovered this lost city more than two centuries ago, but many of its wonders have yet to be revealed.

WHERE: Wadi Musa, Jordan.

HOW TO SEE IT: Petra is a four-hour drive from Amman airport. It's easy to find and signposted in English. Public buses leave regularly from Amman bus station. Wadi Musa is the nearest town, and has a wide selection of accommodation. www.visitjordan.com

TOP TIPS: Come at sunrise or sunset to see the Rose City's colours in all their glory. If you aren't comfortable walking long distances, hire a horse and guide at the visitor centre, near the entrance to the *siq*. Summer temperatures can soar to 40°C (104°F). Come in spring (March to May) or autumn (September to November) instead.

TRY THIS INSTEAD: Mesa Verde National Park in southern Colorado is a spectacular collection of ancient cliff dwellings, cut directly into the sheer rock walls of the surrounding hills. Inhabited by the Ancestral Pueblo people for more than 700 years, between AD 600 and 1300, these precipitous stone villages may not have the grandeur of Petra, but they are nonetheless one of the best-preserved cliff dwellings of the Americas and a remarkable testament to the resourcefulness of the people who built them.
www.nps.gov/meve/index.htm

THE GREAT MOSQUE OF MECCA, SAUDI ARABIA

The Great Mosque of Mecca, al-Masjid al-Ḥarām, is the most important religious site in the Islamic world and the destination for the largest annual pilgrimage on the planet. There are few places that match its cultural significance: 1.6 billion Muslims, one in every five people on Earth, pray in its direction five times a day. More than 2 million people make the journey here each year. It has been one of the most sacred places on Earth for over 1,000 years. Whether or not you're a follower of Islam, Saudi Arabia's Great Mosque is a keystone of global spirituality.

It's also the largest mosque in the world, built to accommodate a staggering 900,000 people, with plans to extend that to nearly 2 million. If you added together the capacity of every premiership football stadium in Great Britain, it wouldn't even reach half the number of people that al-Masjid al-Ḥarām is able to host in a single sitting. Built in the 7th century and then later modified numerous times, the mosque is made up of a central courtyard surrounded by covered prayer areas, comprising a total area of 88 acres. But despite its size, the Great Mosque is really only an outer shell, built for the sole purpose of housing one simple brick building no bigger than a small flat: the Ka'bah.

This 40-foot black cube is the most sacred part of the entire mosque and the spiritual centre of all Muslim life. Legend has it that it was originally built by Adam himself, based on plans handed down directly by God, and then rebuilt by Abraham, the founder of Judaism, Christianity and Islam. The most important part of the Ka'bah is the black stone – a rock that is believed to have fallen directly from heaven and has been worshipped since pre-Islamic times. For many people the chance to touch, or even kiss, this sacred rock is the pinnacle of their religious lives.

Making pilgrimage to Mecca is one of the five pillars of Islam. Known as the Hajj, it takes place over six days during the second week of Dhū al-Hijjah, the final month of the Islamic lunar calendar. Its origins date back to AD 630, when the Prophet Muhammad led a small group of Muslims to the Ka'bah and dedicated the site to the new religion of Islam. Today, all physically and financially able Muslims must complete a pilgrimage to Mecca at least once in their lifetime.

During the Hajj, devotees perform a series of highly controlled and symbolic rituals. Male pilgrims put on the *ihram*, a special white robe that symbolises the equality of all persons before God, irrespective of race, nationality or status. Then the *tawaf* must be performed at least twice – the circling of the Ka'bah seven times – followed by the *sa'y*, in which pilgrims must run back and forth between two nearby small hills. Afterwards, there is a night spent in quiet contemplation under the desert stars, a symbolic stoning of Satan and then an animal is sacrificed as a representation of Abraham's willingness to sacrifice his own son for God.

But the wonder of al-Masjid al-Ḥarām transcends its rituals. Every country, tribe and community of people in the history of the world holds true a belief in something beyond our physical lives. How that is interpreted is, perhaps, less important than the fact that idea exists at all. Whatever you believe, al-Masjid al-Ḥarām is a testament to the power of faith, good and bad.

The Hajj is special too. It is unique among pilgrimages of the world because of its central importance in Islamic life as well as the sheer mass of people, from dozens of

Photo: Wurzelgnohm

countries, which perform it each year. But pilgrimage, as an act in itself, is also one of the great cultural phenomena of our world. From the Christian Way of St James to the Japanese Kumano Kodō, religious traditions around the world have long held the importance of mirroring an inward spiritual journey with an outward physical one. Such separation from our day-to-day lives can intensify the feeling of connection to the divine. And there are secular examples too, from Gandhi's walk to the sea in protest against British rule to Martin Luther King's march on Washington in demand of equal rights. Pilgrimages have power. The Hajj is the greatest on Earth and al-Masjid al-Ḥarām is its final destination.

WHERE: Mecca, Saudi Arabia.

HOW TO SEE IT: Mecca and the al-Masjid al-Ḥarām mosque are open only to Muslims. Numerous tour companies offer package deals around the Hajj. The exact date changes slightly each year.
www.web.haj.gov.sa/english

TOP TIP: Use an approved Saudi travel agent and make sure you obtain an official travel permit before you travel.

TRY THIS INSTEAD: If you're not Muslim but want to experience Islamic art and culture, try the Blue Mosque in Istanbul, Turkey, instead. It's open to tourists and is recognised as one of the most beautiful mosques in the world.
www.bluemosque.co

AFRICA

THE GREAT WILDEBEEST MIGRATION, KENYA AND TANZANIA

The annual wildebeest migration, across the Serengeti in Tanzania and parts of the Maasai Mara in Kenya, is the largest migration of land animals on the planet. An average of 1.5 million make the 1,000-mile circular journey every year. And though the wildebeest are the star, they are accompanied by more than 350,000 gazelle, 200,000 zebra as well as thousands of eland, antelope and impala. Herds stretch 25 miles long, filling the entire horizon. Galloping hooves kick up the dusty ground into a storm of earthen mist. The ground shakes. The noise is like thunder. This is Africa's great migration. Seeing it is one the greatest spectacles on Earth.

The wildebeest's journey is hard and fraught with danger. The story begins on the slopes of the Ngorongoro Crater in the south-eastern corner of the Serengeti Plains. Between January and March the wildebeest cows give birth to their young in near perfect unison. Within three weeks, more than 300,000 calves will take their first steps. Dozens of lions and hundreds of hyenas stalk the peripheries of the herd, looking for easy prey. But such abundance satiates the predators and ensures the maximum amount of young will survive. The newborns are also highly adaptive, gaining coordination faster than any other ungulate. Within two minutes a newborn calf is on its feet. Within five it can run with the herd.

By the end of March the short grass of the southern Serengeti is wearing thin and the wildebeest begin their journey west in search of food. Their movement is triggered by an awareness of environmental factors. They are sensitive to changes in atmospheric pressure and humidity, allowing them to sense the onset of distant rain, and on the horizon thunderclouds begin to bellow, providing a visual stimulus too. Where the rains are, grass will grow; and so they move.

And they are built to travel. Although 3,000 lions, 1,000 leopards, 300 cheetahs, packs of wild dogs and untold hyena await them, they are ready. A fully grown wildebeest is eight feet long, 600 pounds and able to run at 40 mph. They have evolved to cover long distances quickly and economically. And while predators are confined to small territories and sprints, the herds can keep up a steady pace and simply blast through.

As the rains set in, the herds travel north-west through woodland and low hills towards Lake Victoria and the plains of the Serengeti's western corridor. Here, in May and June, usually at a full moon, the rut begins, accompanied by vicious fighting between dominant males.

Then they head north, towards fresh grass into Kenya and the Maasai Mara Game Reserve. But to get there they face one of the greatest obstacles of their entire journey: rivers. For most of the year the Mbalageti and the Grumeti Rivers in the Serengeti and the Mara River in Kenya are placid. But sudden rainfall can create violent torrents. It is not uncommon for 5,000 wildebeest to drown in a single crossing if the conditions are unfavourable. But that's the least of their problems. Waiting beneath the depths are giant Nile crocodiles, fourteen feet long with jaws that can snap a neck in seconds.

But the Promised Land is on the other side. During the course of their migration, 250,000 wildebeest will die before reaching the lush grasslands of the Maasai Mara – from predators, thirst, starvation and just pure exhaustion. Once there, the giant herds spend months feeding and fattening up. But by late October, as the first rains begin to hit the distant Serengeti, once again filling seasonal waterholes and flushing the ground with grass, they begin to close the circle. The herd treks south, cows heavy with the new season's young, back to where they started, on the slopes of the Ngorongoro Crater. Here they feed, wait for their young to be born and watch the horizon for thunderclouds to light up the sky once more.

In reality there is no single event of the migration. The wildebeest are the migration: a constant movement across the plains of Africa, chasing rainbows in search of food. Their movement is the lifeblood of the plains, cropping grass, fertilising the land and providing vital protein for predators. They face many obstacles, but now there is a new threat too. East African population booms have resulted in development pressures, deforestation, poaching and habitat fragmentation. Climate change is causing more intense periods of rain and drought. All this threatens the clockwork balance of life on Africa's great plains. And the great migration is the keystone of the entire ecosystem. If the wildebeest should fall, the Serengeti will fall with it. This may be one of the greatest spectacles on Earth, but it's also one of the most vivid examples of the interconnectedness of life. Everything depends on everything else. There is no migration in its singularity. Only a dance, a symphony with different players and many parts. Africa's great migration is as much a journey as it is the music of the planet itself.

WHERE: Serengeti National Park, Tanzania, and Maasai Mara National Park, Kenya.

HOW TO SEE IT: Time your visit with the migration cycles of the wildebeest, but cross your fingers too: the exact dates of the migration depend on the rain and vary each year. July to October is generally the best time to go to Kenya. January to March is calving season around the Ngorongoro Crater in Tanzania, while April to June the herds travel through the central and western Serengeti.
www.serengeti.org
www.magicalkenya.com

TOP TIPS: The Mara River crossing is probably the most spectacular event of the entire migration. Come between July and November for the best chance of seeing it, but you'll need patience and luck. If you can afford it, stay in a private game reserve just outside the National Park's boundary where there are fewer crowds and more intimate wildlife encounters. Or even better, book a private mobile camp, which follows the herds.

TRY THIS INSTEAD: Each year, as many as half a million caribou migrate hundreds of miles between their winter ranges in northern Alaska and the Yukon to their traditional calving grounds on the Arctic Refuge's coastal plain. Seeing it is one of the greatest wildlife shows in North America.
www.canada.travel

THE SAHARA DESERT, NORTH AFRICA

The Sahara is the largest hot desert on the planet. Antarctica and the Arctic are bigger, but they are cold deserts. For the classic view of a scorching, barren land, laden with giant windswept sand dunes and arid rocky crags, the Sahara simply cannot be beaten. And it is still immense. At 3.6 million square miles, it engulfs more than 30 per cent of the African continent, covering large sections of Algeria, Chad, Egypt, Libya, Mali, Mauritania, Morocco, Niger, Sudan and Tunisia. It is roughly 40 times the size of Great Britain and three times the size of India. It would nearly cover the entire USA. Spread it out across Europe and only the edges would be spared.

But the size of the Sahara is only part of its wonder. The real magic is how the desert makes you feel. In the day the sands sing like cellos, an orchestra of rolling grains that vibrate in synchrony. At night, the Milky Way glows in pure darkness like a living, breathing thing. The land is pure, clean, swept free. There is liberation here, an emptiness that quietens the soul.

Its terrain is varied. Seas of giant sand dunes, called ergs, cover roughly 20 per cent of its total area. They reach 500 feet high and shift in ever-changing patterns of wind. Dusty gravelly plains, known as regs – the remains of a dried-out prehistoric seabed – cover 70 per cent. There are high plateaus and mountains: the Atlas range across Morocco and Tunisia, the Tibesti of southern Libya and Chad. And there are even cities too: Cairo, Tripoli and Timbuktu all fall within the Sahara's boundaries.

And its power is humbling. Hurricane winds spin up sand storms and scour everything in their path. In the

Photo: Wonker

day, temperatures regularly soar over 40°C. The highest ever recorded here was 58°C (136°F). But at night the thermometer plummets. All memory of warmth disappears, the ground freezes to −6°C (22°F). The Sahara is an alien land. We have no right to be here. And should we venture in, the clock is ticking on our demise.

But yet we do. People have long been drawn to the danger and sheer desolate beauty of the Sahara. Marco Polo crossed parts of it in the 13th century. Lawrence of Arabia used it to outwit the Turks in the First World War. Explorers, kings, treasure hunters, traders have all met their fortune here, and their fate.

But where most would perish, there are a few who thrive. Bedouins, nomadic people of the desert, have survived in the Sahara for thousands of years. They rely on underground aquifers, natural wells that pump water to the surface, creating sudden vibrant oases of date trees, ponds and fruits. Crops grow, animals flourish and cities are built, entirely on the foundations of these few precious drops.

And the Sahara has another life-giver too. The River Nile cuts across its eastern edge, from north to south through Egypt and Sudan. It is the longest river in the world and perhaps the most important too. It is here in the fertile Nile Valley, surrounded by barren inhospitable mountains and plains on all sides, that the first flourishes of human civilisation began.

Perhaps that's the real wonder of the Sahara. Antoine de Saint-Exupéry, author of *The Little Prince*, said: 'What makes the desert beautiful is that somewhere it hides a well.' The desert represents the beginning, and the end, of everything. It is the pinnacle of the pendulum swing. The Sahara was a lush and fertile land 10,000 years ago. Prehistoric rock paintings depict cattle, giraffe, elephants and lions. But then sometime around 6,000 years ago the climate shifted. The rains stopped and the grassland retreated – it is suspected with alarming speed – and all living things either left or died and disappeared. It is a reminder of how fragile the balance of life is. But it's a reminder of how enduring it is too. Even in the depths of this desert silence, the sands still sing. Even in the harshest drought, flowers will grow.

WHERE: North Africa.

HOW TO SEE IT: The Sahara has a huge variety of terrain, but to experience the classic desert of endless windswept sand dunes head to the Drâa Valley in south-eastern Morocco. From the town of M'Hamid, it's easy to pick up day trips and overnight excursions into the Erg Chigaga, a stunning 25-mile ribbon of dunes. The fierce heat of summer is dangerous. Visit between October and April for the best temperatures, but be aware that winter nights can be freezing. Sand storms are possible January to May.

TOP TIPS: Make sure to spend a night out in the desert: the stars and silence are unlike anything else on Earth. Check government warnings before travel. Some of the most spectacular locations, for example the Ahaggar and Tassili mountain ranges of Algeria, were off-limits at the time of writing.

TRY THIS INSTEAD: The Arabian Desert is the second largest hot desert in the world. Covering large parts of the Arabian Peninsula, it's known for its beautiful sand dunes and desolate scenery. Oman is a safe, friendly and beautiful base from which to see it.
www.omantourism.gov.om

THE GREAT PYRAMID OF GIZA, EGYPT

There is no monument on Earth that represents the mystery, awe and sheer magnificence of a world wonder better than the Great Pyramid of Giza. Built more than 4,500 years ago, it is the oldest of the original seven wonders of the ancient world and the only one still standing today. Located on the outskirts of Cairo in Egypt, it was 481 feet tall at the time of its construction, with four 755-foot sides, and it is still one of the largest man-made structures ever built. If you were to hollow it out, it would be big enough to hold the cathedrals of Florence, Milan, St Peter's, Westminster Abbey and St Paul's combined. For nearly 4,000 years, until the spire of Lincoln Cathedral was fashioned in 1311, it was the tallest building in the world.

Today, it is probably the most recognisable landmark on the planet, but it is filled with mystery too. The inside has barely been explored, the purpose of it is still under debate and the technical wizardry required for its construction has baffled archaeologists for centuries. Even now, with all our sophisticated tools, cranes and computers, building it would pose a formidable challenge. And the truth is, no one's exactly sure how they did it.

The Great Pyramid is thought to have been an elaborate tomb for its king, the Pharaoh Khufu, who built it between 2584 BC and 2561 BC. Nearby are two smaller pyramids built by successive pharaohs over the next decades – the second by Khufu's son, Khafre, and the third, and smallest, by Menkaure. At the time of its construction, the Great Pyramid was encased in a sheath of dazzling limestone, which has since been looted, but it would have once glittered in the sunlight for hundreds of miles around.

The method of its construction is still a hotly contested debate. Despite the engineering and logistical problems involved, historical accounts record that Khufu's Great Pyramid took little over twenty years to complete. According to some calculations, such a feat would have required fitting one enormous limestone block, of which there were about 2.3 million, into place roughly every two to five minutes. And every single one of those, each weighing between two and a half and fifteen tonnes, had to be quarried, cut to precision and transported over 500 miles using specially constructed sledges. Then once the stones were on site, they had to somehow be hauled up as much as 203 levels, or courses, the equivalent of a 40-storey building.

It seems impossible, but a new theory has an answer. It turns out the pyramid may have in fact been built from the inside out via a system of levers and a spiralling internal ramp. In this view the builders began by building around the burial chamber in the centre and simply worked backwards and upwards from there, layer by layer, until the four corner stones were reached. As for the outer casing stones, recent microscopic examination of their chemical make-up shows a slightly different composition to nearby limestone supplies, suggesting that these stones were not quarried, carved and transported at all, but were rather casted on site using a kind of ancient earth-based cement.

But the truth is no one knows for sure. What we do know is that they were built by a combination of ingenuity, hard work and massive amounts of manpower. The Greek historian Herodotus claimed the Great Pyramid was constructed by a slave army, 100,000 strong. Modern archaeologists see evidence of a smaller, but more skilled, force of 20,000 permanent workers, who lived in a nearby city. Such an undertaking required enormous bureaucratic power. The

Photo: Hedwig Storch

workers had to be housed and fed. The administrators had to coordinate the supply of stone, rope, wood and fuel. This drove them to advance their civilisation and technical understanding at a staggering rate. The ancient Egyptians may have built the pyramids, but in a very real way the pyramids built ancient Egypt too.

And the level of precision they achieved is astonishing. The four corners of the pyramid are aligned to the four cardinal directions to within three arcminutes' accuracy of true north, a feat that could not be achieved without a deep understanding of astronomy. The thirteen-acre site was levelled to within one inch of variation. The burial chamber is built to the exact proportions of phi, the golden ratio. The outer casings were fastened with such mastery that a razor blade could not be inserted between them.

But the real wonders may still be hidden within. Inside is Khufu's burial chamber, built of huge blocks of solid red granite and decorated with inscriptions and scenes of life in ancient Egypt. Surrounding these is a series of ascending and descending passageways, ventilation shafts, a 26-foot high Grand Gallery, ante-rooms, subterranean vaults and what is known as the Queen's chamber, thought to be another burial room used for his wife. It is, by far, the most elaborate internal network that has ever been seen within a pyramid.

And yet we've barely scratched the surface. In 2014, a robot was steered down one hitherto inaccessible passage and beamed back images of mysterious miniature doors and cavity openings sealed with enormous granite plugs. Archaeologists have been prevented from digging within, for fear of causing damage, but more advanced techniques may soon change that. At the time of writing scientists were using sub-atomic scanners to search for hidden vaults and chambers. And they have good reason to be hopeful. The known internal spaces within the Great Pyramid occupy only an estimated 0.01 per cent of its total volume. Even accounting for separating and supporting blocks there may still be hundreds of rooms yet to discover.

And that's what makes the Great Pyramid so special. It may be the oldest man-made wonder on this list, but there are still questions unanswered, there are still mysteries to be revealed. How did copper tools, the only ones the Egyptians had at their disposal, cut blocks of limestone and granite – a task difficult even for the equivalent iron and steel tools we use today? Why was there such a sudden and rapid improvement in technical expertise from the previous century's work? And why was such technical mastery never repeated? Why did Khufu's historians not leave more account of his great work in their inscriptions, while so much of the rest of his story is told? Historical texts claim the outer casing, before it was looted, was covered in symbols. What did they say? Perhaps we'll find out soon, perhaps we'll never know. But contemplating those mysteries is part of the joy of wonder itself.

WHERE: Giza, Egypt.

HOW TO SEE IT: Avoid the summer months when the heat is unbearable and the pollution of Cairo is at its worst. October into early November is not yet peak season, but the temperatures are manageable. March and April are good times too, but avoid the Easter break when visitor numbers soar. A limited number of tickets to see inside the Great Pyramid of Khufu are sold on a first come, first served basis, on site, at 8am and 1pm every day. Arrive as early as possible for the best chance. If you miss out, try the neighbouring Pyramid of Chephren instead, where tickets are available

throughout the day. Check the status of government warnings before travelling.
www.egypt.travel

TOP TIPS: For the best views, head to a rocky escarpment two and a half miles south of the Pyramid of Menkaure. Be mindful of aggressive touts and guides while on site; haggle for everything.

TRY THIS INSTEAD: Luxor, the former ancient city of Thebes and capital of Egypt, has some of the most spectacular archaeological sites in the country. Don't miss the Temple of Karnak, the Valley of the Kings, the Valley of the Queens and the tomb of Tutankhamun. Dawn balloon rides over the valley are spectacular.

VICTORIA FALLS, ZAMBIA AND ZIMBABWE

Victoria Falls is the largest singular waterfall in the world. Angel Falls in Venezuela is taller. Iguaçu in Brazil and Argentina is wider. But taking all dimensions together, Victoria produces the largest single curtain of falling water on the planet.

And surely the most beautiful too. Located on the Zambezi River, on the border between Zambia and Zimbabwe, close to 300,000 gallons of water pour over the lip of this enormous gorge every second – in a single minute, the Falls would fill 26 Olympic-sized swimming pools. Spray shoots 1,000 feet in the air and can be seen from twenty miles away. Its mist sparkles with iridescent rainbows. Lush forests of mahogany, fig and palm trees blanket its banks. Falcons and black eagles soar overhead. Victoria Falls is nature at its most powerful, awe-inspiring and sublime.

The local Kololo tribe has known of its existence for thousands of years. To them it is Mosi-oa-Tunya, the Smoke that Thunders. The name Victoria was given to the Falls by the British explorer David Livingstone in 1855, during his expedition up the Zambezi.

His story is the stuff of legend. As a missionary, he dedicated his life to the exploration of Africa and achieved many great feats. He crossed the Kalahari Desert, charted vast swathes of the Zambezi River, travelled up the Nile, survived a mauling by a lion and became the first European to cross the width of the African continent in its entirety. In doing so, he introduced African culture to the rest of the world and became a prominent spokesman against slavery, playing a key role in its eventual demise. But the discovery, in European terms, of this spectacular waterfall was undoubtedly one of his crowning achievements. 'No one can imagine the beauty of the view from anything witnessed in England', he would later write. 'Scenes so lovely must have been gazed upon by angels in their flight.'

The waterfall itself was formed due to the wearing down of soft sandstone cracks in the hard basalt plateau over which the Zambezi flows. For 2 million years, the river has torn away at this softer stone, creating a series of dramatic zigzagging gorges that bubble turbulent rapids like a boiling pot. At the first drop, Victoria Falls itself, the Zambezi is more than a mile wide and falls 355 feet at its peak.

And its power is formidable. Local tribes believe that the river god Nyaminyami inhabits the Zambezi and the area around the Falls. Legend has it that in 1958 when the Kariba dam was being built upriver, he rose in anger.

Photo: Florence Devouard

On that day the river elevated eighteen feet, the flow rate increased from an average of just over 38,000 cubic feet per second to almost 25 million cubic feet per second and simply destroyed everything in its path. Whether or not you believe the legend, to stand beneath Victoria Falls is to look the ferocity of nature in the eye, to see, in a single glance, its unfathomable strength and its indescribable beauty.

WHERE: Livingstone, Zambia, and Victoria Falls, Zimbabwe.

HOW TO SEE IT: The Falls are located on the border between southern Zambia and northern Zimbabwe. The Zimbabwe side has about three-quarters of the Falls, most of the viewpoints and the better facilities. But to get close you need to go to the Zambian side. The border crossing is easy and most tourists choose to see both sides.

TOP TIPS: Come in the dry season, October to December, to experience one of the most unique thrills in the world. At the Devil's Pool, a natural swimming hole on the edge of the Falls, an underwater rock barrier makes it possible to swim right up to the lip of the thundering cascade without fear of being swept away.

TRY THIS INSTEAD: Iguaçu Falls, on the Brazil–Argentinian border, is a chain of 275 individual cascades that stretches for nearly two miles. It is one of the world's great natural wonders and a near miss for this book.
www.brazil.org.za
www.iguazuargentina.com

THE GREAT RIFT VALLEY, EAST AFRICA

Stretching 4,000 miles across East Africa, from Jordan to Mozambique, Africa's Great Rift Valley is one of the most biodiverse places on Earth. Mountain gorillas, lions and rhino make their home here. Enormous herds of wildebeest and zebra walk its plains. Its borders contain the Great Lakes of Africa, including Tanganyika, the second deepest and largest by volume in the world (4,823 feet and 4,500 cubic miles, respectively) and Victoria, the southern source of the Nile. From outer space, it is the most significant physical detail of our planet. But the wonder of the Great Rift Valley goes beyond its description. It is known as the 'cradle of mankind'. The oldest known fossil records of our most ancient ancestors were found here and their story is rewriting everything we know about ourselves and where we come from. To be in the Great Rift Valley is to return to the source, to glimpse our deep past and understand, in an instant, the long road that we have travelled.

It began forming about 20 million years ago when the Arabian, African-Nubian and African-Somalian tectonic plates started pulling apart, creating a vast fracture, or rift, along these intersecting fault lines. This process represents the first stage in the creation of new continents and oceans, and it's not finished yet. Pressure from deep under the Earth's crust will eventually split the horn of Africa along this line, causing it to break off and form a new island with a new ocean in between. These enormous but near invisible forces shape our world. And nowhere on Earth are they more clearly seen.

The results are spectacular. As the African continent separated from Saudi Arabia, deep cracks formed in the

Earth's surface, which filled with water creating some of the largest lakes in the world. Huge diversity of birdlife inhabits them, including 4 million bright pink Lesser Flamingos, one of the world's great wildlife spectacles. Ancient volcanoes dot the landscape: the ice-clad summits of Mount Kilimanjaro and Mount Kenya as well as the 102-square-mile extinct caldera of the Ngorongoro Crater, one of the most wildlife-rich habitats on the planet. There are hot springs and geysers, wetlands, woodlands, deserts and swamps. And in the vast rolling grasslands of the Maasai Mara, the largest concentration of big herbivores and predators on Earth.

But there is something even more special too. These geologic processes are responsible for creating the climatic, and wildlife-rich, conditions that caused our ancestors to leave the forest, walk upright and, eventually, learn to read books like this and contemplate the wonders of the world. Our journey began here. And, crucially, the conditions here are also perfect to preserve those evolutionary changes. Especially in the Olduvai Gorge of northern Tanzania and the Afar Desert of Ethiopia, where the fossils of thousands of ancient hominins, or early humans, have been discovered.

The most famous is Lucy, a near intact *Australopithecus* skeleton that is 3.2 million years old. When she was alive, she would have been just over three feet tall, and 60 pounds, with a slender body. Her brain was not much bigger than a modern chimpanzee, but she already walked upright, as a human, and no longer had an opposable big toe, like an ape. Many other specimens have been found in the region, some even older, but none as complete. That's important because it enables scientists to envision how she moved and lived, which helps to paint a vivid picture of our own evolutionary history. Upon her discovery, she was immediately hailed as the oldest direct ancestor of modern human beings. But there may well be older, still waiting to be uncovered.

The Great Rift Valley is a wonder of the world on a number of counts: geologically, biologically and, perhaps, just for sheer beauty alone. But its central place in uncovering the history of humankind sets it apart. Our story began here and it is here that we may well finally piece it all together. The future is not yet written, but in the Great Rift Valley we are reminded of how far we've come. Darwin said it best: 'Man may be excused for feeling some pride at having risen … to the very summit of the organic scale; and the fact of his having thus risen, instead of having been aboriginally placed there, may give him hope for a still higher destiny in the distant future.'

WHERE: East Africa.

HOW TO SEE IT: The Serengeti, Ngorongoro Crater and Olduvai Gorge can be easily combined into a single trip. June to September is the dry season and offers the best opportunities for wildlife viewing. April and May have the fewest crowds. Booking through a reputable tour operator is often the best option.
www.ngorongorocrater.org
www.serengeti.org
www.olduvai-gorge.org

TOP TIP: Time your trip with the great wildebeest migration – see chapter for details.

TRY THIS INSTEAD: The Sterkfontein Caves, 30 miles north-west of Johannesburg in South Africa, lay claim to being another cradle of humankind, with numerous early hominid

Photo: Woodhouse

fossils discovered here. Combine with the spectacular wildlife viewing of Kruger National Park, 280 miles west.

www.maropeng.co.za

www.sanparks.org/parks/kruger

THE GREAT MOSQUE OF DJENNÉ, MALI

The Great Mosque of Djenné in Mali, West Africa, is the largest mud brick structure in the world and one of the African continent's most striking architectural achievements. It's one of the most unusual too. Sculpted up directly from the dusty brown earth like a desert mirage, this sandcastle-like 50-foot high place of worship is the pinnacle of Sudano-Sahelian structural design and a masterpiece of adobe-style building.

But the Djenné Mosque is not just a relic. As climate change drives us to search for more sustainable ways to construct our homes and cities, it is also a testament to the architectural vision that can be achieved using only natural and renewable materials. It may be an example of one of our earliest, and most simple, forms of construction, but the Great Mosque of Djenné is also an inspiration for what our future may hold.

The city of Djenné, on the floodlands of the Niger and Bani Rivers, 300 miles south-west of Timbuktu, is the oldest known city in sub-Saharan Africa, founded in AD 800 near the site of an even older city that had been inhabited since 250 BC. In the 15th and 16th centuries, it was a place of great trade. The site of the Djenné Mosque was originally a 13th-century palace that was later converted. But by the 19th century, that building was considered too lavish for the humility required of worship and was demolished. What stands today was built over 100 years ago, between 1906 and 1909, and is made entirely from local mud and palm wood.

Given the simplicity of the raw material, the complexity of its design is staggering. Built on a raised plinth to protect it from seasonal floods, 245 feet across on each side, the outer façade is constructed of sun-baked mud bricks, held together by mud mortar and plastered over with mud. The finish is smooth and rounded, like a clay figurine. Thick palm wood poles jut out from each side, like spearheads. Three box-like minaret towers spire upwards, topped by ostrich egg crowns, with spiral stairways inside. There are buttressed ramparts, like a fortress balustrade, with portcullis windows and moulded columns streaming down to the ground. Half the mosque is covered by a roof, supported by palm wood columns and can accommodate as many as 3,000 people, the other half is an open-air prayer area surrounded by an arcade of vaulted archways. The whole building blends into the ground with exquisite balance and accord, as if it is an extension of the earth itself.

And it is being continually built. Each year the people of Djenné come together in an annual festival, called the *Crepissage de la Grand Mosquée*, in which they re-plaster and fix parts of the building. Drums beat as the men perch perilously from the protruding wood poles, like a makeshift scaffold. Young girls carry bowls of mud and water from the riverbed. Women pound millet and make pancakes. Barefoot boys churn vats at their feet. It is the biggest party of the year. But by participating, each generation also adds its subtle mark, helping to evolve the mosque like a living part of the community itself.

Mud and raw earth have been used as building materials by indigenous communities across the world for thousands of

Photo: BluesyPete

years. Today, it is estimated that 40–50 per cent of the world's population still live in earthen structures. It is widespread because there is a natural harmony between construction materials and the environment. But it's functional too; adobe buildings provide efficient insulation that keeps the interior cool and pleasant even in the fiercest of climates.

And although it may be one of the oldest forms of human construction, there is a collective wisdom from its use that we can still learn from. Earthen architecture creates little waste, requires minimal energy consumption and is easy to maintain and recycle. The modern production of cement for building is known to account for more than 5 per cent of global carbon dioxide emissions. Profound changes in the way we construct our cities and homes will need to be made in the coming decades. The Great Mosque of Djenné is a unique architectural wonder, and one of the great landmarks of Africa, but it is also a unique reminder of where we come from and an inspiration for where we may one day still return.

WHERE: Djenné, Mali.

HOW TO SEE IT: If travelling independently, it's easiest to get a taxi from the nearby city of Mopti, about two hours away. August and September, after the rainy season, can be one of the most picturesque times to visit. The festival of plastering is held in May each year. Non-Muslims are currently not allowed inside the Great Mosque. www.djennetourism.com

TOP TIPS: Don't miss the Grand Marché, a market held every Monday in town. It's filled with thousands of traders from all over the region and is considered one of the most colourful markets in Africa. Check government warnings before travelling to Mali. Booking with a reputable tour operator can be a good option.

TRY THIS INSTEAD: The rock-hewn churches of Lalibela in Ethiopia are another, equally impressive, African landmark. Chiselled directly from the volcanic rock beds surrounding the town, these eleven 13th-century buildings are also rightly regarded as one of the great architectural wonders of the continent.
www.ethiopia.travel

ASIA

THE GREAT WALL OF CHINA

The Great Wall of China is a 13,000-mile network of walled fortifications that extends across the country's northern territory. Built over two millennia by the hands of millions of workers, it is the longest man-made structure on the planet. But it is not a continuous wall, nor was it conceived as a singular vision. Rather the Great Wall, or Chángchéng, the Long Wall as it is known in China, is like the tributary of a river, a vast earth and stone snake with multiple arms and legs that stretches across the nation from Shanhaiguan in Hebei province in the east, to Jiayuguan in Gansu province in the west. That it is the only man-made structure that can be seen from space is a myth. Its natural building materials blend into the local topography making it, in fact, incredibly hard to discern, even from low Earth orbit. But the scale of it is nonetheless astonishing.

The idea was originally conceived by the Emperor Qin Shi Huang in the 3rd century BC. Up until this point, China was composed of a number of separate, and often warring, kingdoms. As the first ruler of a unified China, Qin Shi Huang ordered that the scattered fortifications of these smaller provinces be joined together into a single continuous wall, which would protect the empire from Mongol and barbarian raiders to the north. This enormous barrier was known as the 10,000-Li-Long Wall (a *li* being a Chinese unit of distance equivalent to about a third of a mile) and would stretch from the Tibetan plateau in the west to the Pacific.

Construction on the wall continued on and off through the centuries as emperors, and enemies, rose and fell. But it reached its peak during the Ming dynasty of 1368–1644. Despite the more than 1,500 years of previous effort, the Mongol hordes, under Genghis Khan and his son Kublai, managed to breach the Great Wall in the middle of the 13th century and subsequently ruled over China until 1368. After they were overthrown, in fear of another attack, the new Ming rulers ceaselessly strengthened and maintained the Great Wall for three centuries, expanding it to over 5,500 miles of continuous fortification. At its peak, more than a million soldiers were posted along its ramparts.

Most of what still stands today is a result of their effort. The materials shifted from rammed earth, adobe and stone to carefully casted bricks. The wall stood on average 23 feet high and 21 feet wide. Small openings along the barricades allowed archers to fire on invaders, while larger holes further down were used to drop stones and other weapons. Signal towers were built on hilltops and clear vantage points along the wall, so that fires and smoke signals could be used to communicate with garrisons stationed further down the watch. Enormous passes, major castle-like strongholds within the walls, were placed at key strategic points and along the intersection of trade routes. By the time the Ming Dynasty had finished its work, the Great Wall snaked across the entire length of China's northern reach, across deserts, forests, deep gorges and over rugged mountain peaks, like the spine of an enormous stone dragon.

But the cost was high. It is estimated that, in total, 1 million people died in order to see the Great Wall built – from accidents, hunger and exhaustion; their bones, it is rumoured, are buried inside the wall itself. The struggle was enormous too. Hundreds of thousands of peasants, alongside soldiers and convicts, were forcibly sent to work. Mass graves lie beside the foundations, as if the wall was, in fact, a long, stretched out tombstone marking the largest cemetery ever built.

But their achievement will last through the aeons of time. The Great Wall has become a symbol for China itself. Built as a means of military defence, it has transcended its original purpose and is now an emblem of the country's enduring strength and long-sighted vision. Taking all of its branches together, the Great Wall of China would stretch more than halfway around the circumference of the world. It would take years to walk its entire length. There is, perhaps, no more audacious project ever undertaken in the history of human civilisation. And none that have cost more in time and lives to realise.

WHERE: Northern China.

HOW TO SEE IT: Beijing is the best base to see the most popular sections (but see Top Tips below). Badaling, about

Photo: Doyleconan

42 miles from the city, is beautifully restored and the most convenient and popular section, with all the amenities, crowds and developments that go along with it. Mutianyu, 30 miles east of Badaling, is arguably just as beautiful, but with fewer crowds. Jinshanling, about three hours from the city, is wilder, quieter and offers some of the best hiking. Buses are complicated and there are no trains. If not joining an organised tour, the best bet is to either hire a car or get a taxi. For a real adventure, join a multi-day trek along rarely seen sections, camping out in abandoned watchtowers each night. Autumn has mild temperatures, smaller crowds and golden leaves.

www.cnto.org

TOP TIPS: If visiting one of the popular sections, avoid weekends and holidays. Consider staying overnight at one of the nearby hotels in order to beat the crowds and watch the sunrise, and spectacular sunset, over the Great Wall.

TRY THIS INSTEAD: Though nowhere near the same scale or spectacle, Hadrian's Wall in northern England was built for similar purposes, here by the Romans in AD 117, to defend against the marauding Scottish Picts. Stretching 73 miles, coast-to-coast, from the River Tyne in the east to Bowness-on-Solway in the west, it is one of the best preserved of the ancient Roman frontiers.

www.english-heritage.org.uk

MOUNT EVEREST, NEPAL

Mount Everest is more than just the tallest mountain on Earth: it's the ultimate symbol of the human spirit for adventure and exploration. That we risk our lives to stand on the roof of the world is more than foolish vanity. As Mallory said: we climb it 'because it's there', because to reach beyond our grasp, to dare to look into the abode of the gods, is what makes us human and what has carried us so far.

The mountain has many names. The Tibetans call it Chomolungma, 'Goddess Mother of the World'. In Sanskrit, it is referred to as Sagarmatha, the 'Peak of Heaven'. It is located right on the border between Tibet and Nepal, deep in the Himalayan range, the tallest, most formidable, mountain range on Earth. This towering pyramidal peak stretches an almost unimaginable 29,029 feet into the sky – high enough to touch the tip of the jet stream and peer into the darkness beyond the stratosphere.

The summit is not fit for human life. Temperatures never rise above freezing, even in summer, and can plummet to –60°C. Storms strike without warning. Avalanches regularly thunder down the slopes. Winds can reach 175 mph. Breathing is nearly impossible. At the top, one-third of the amount of oxygen is absorbed into the blood compared to as at sea level. Take someone from the ground to the summit, without acclimatisation, and they would be unconscious in minutes and dead soon after.

And, on Everest, death is always close at hand: nearly 300 people have lost their lives here. In the worst year, 1996, fifteen climbers died in a single season. For every twenty that attempt the summit, one will never return. And more than 100 corpses still litter the slopes today: the conditions are

Photo: Rdevany

simply too dangerous, and the climbers too exhausted, to carry the dead home.

But still we are drawn to it. The first ascent was by Sir Edmund Hillary and Tenzing Norgay on 29 May 1953. It made world headlines and the pair were celebrated across the globe. But they may have been beaten to the post. George Mallory and Andrew Irvine made an attempt on the north-east ridge nearly 30 years earlier. They were last seen climbing high and strong near the summit before a snowstorm blew in and they simply disappeared. It would be 75 years before Mallory's body was found; Irvine's is still missing. They left no evidence on the summit that they had made it. But Irving had a camera and that film may tell a different story. What happened to his body, and what those images may contain, continues to be one of the great mysteries of mountaineering history.

Since then there have been incredible feats. In 1978, Reinhold Messner became the first person to climb the mountain without oxygen, an achievement that was thought, at the time, to be biologically impossible. Two years later he did it again, this time solo. The youngest person to reach the top was thirteen-year-old Malavath Poorna, a farm-girl from India, raised in poverty; the oldest, 80-year-old Yuichiro Miura, from Japan. Everest has now been skied, snowboarded, paraglided over and there's even been a wedding on top.

But perhaps the greatest feat of all is performed by the indigenous people of the Himalayas, the Sherpas, each year. Centuries living at altitude has given them an almost superhuman strength in the mountains. While we struggle, they carry load after load of equipment. Many have summited numerous times. But even more important is the way they do it. The mountain is sacred to them. Each expedition begins with the *puja*, a ceremony in which they ask for permission to pass. Rather than seeking to conquer the mountain, they ask for communion instead.

For those seeking to make the summit, it begins like this: staring up from Base Camp at the enormous face, listening to avalanches and the low moans of glaciers shifting beneath your feet. First, you must cross the Khumbu Icefall, a dangerous labyrinth of hidden crevasses and falling ice pinnacles that has claimed more lives than anywhere else on the mountain. Then you reach Camp 1, 20,000 feet high, close enough to touch the face of Everest for the first time. But the altitude is beginning to attack your body, raging headaches pound your skull. From here it is a slow, silent march to Camp 2, 1,000 feet higher, clouds rolling in to the valley below. And then further on, step after agonising step to Camp 3, as precarious as an eagle's nest with thousand-foot drops on each side and falling blocks of ice racing down around you. At Camp 4 you are in the death zone, 26,000 feet. The sky is dark, the wall is steep, everyone is afraid. The final push begins in the middle of the night, a row of headlamps snaking upwards into the endless black. After what seems like an eternity, the first rays of dawn arrive, a thin blue line that brings light but no warmth. You are dizzy, your fingers are numb, your heart is beating faster than it ever has in your life. A mistake here means death. But then suddenly, there is nowhere else to go. You see the north face falling off before you, a flag in front and, if you're lucky, a friend to hug and hold. Congratulations, you are standing on the roof of the world.

WHERE: Sagarmatha National Park, Nepal.

HOW TO SEE IT: Reaching the summit of Everest is incredibly dangerous, expensive and requires supreme levels

of fitness. Choose a reputable operator, prepare thoroughly, take no chances and be aware of the risks. April and May are the best window for climbing. If you want to see the mountain, but keep your feet on the ground, take a trek to base camp instead: it offers many of the best views, and the chance to soak up the unique culture and wildlife of the region, but with a fraction of the risks.
www.welcomenepal.com

TOP TIPS: Namche Bazaar and Tengboche are two of the best locations for photographing Mount Everest; both are passed on the trek to Base Camp. Shoot early before the clouds roll in.

TRY THIS INSTEAD: It's now possible to climb Everest in virtual reality. Sólfar Studios are scheduled to release 'Everest VR' in 2016. Early demos have proven too realistic and scary for many reviewers to handle.
www.solfar.com

THE TAJ MAHAL, INDIA

The Taj Mahal is, perhaps, the most sublimely beautiful building ever constructed. Built by the Shah Jahan on the banks of the Yamuna River in northern India, this enormous white marble mausoleum is the final resting place of his third wife, the Persian princess Arjumand Bano Begum. Shah Jahan ruled from 1627 to 1658, at the peak of the Mughal empire's power, a dynasty that controlled most of northern India from the early 16th to the mid-18th centuries. But, in the wealth of his entire kingdom, Arjumand was his greatest treasure of all. Poets said that in her presence the moon would hide its face in shame, such was the greatness of her beauty. He called her Mumtaz Mahal, 'Chosen One of the Palace', and from the day they were married she never left his side. But in 1631, after giving birth to their fourteenth child, his beloved died. On her deathbed he promised to build her the most beautiful tomb the world had ever seen. That tomb he called the Taj Mahal, an abbreviation of her name. And he kept his word.

Work started immediately. It took 22 years, with more than 20,000 workers conscripted from across India, Persia, Europe and the Ottoman empire: labourers, architects, masons, stonecutters, painters and artists. One thousand elephants were brought in to haul the enormous marble blocks needed for construction, each one weighing in excess of two tonnes, from quarries 200 miles away. It cost 32 million rupees, or roughly US$1 billion in today's money. But while he ploughed his empire's entire resources into this singular task, the people suffered. There was famine in the land. Farmers needed infrastructure and support, but what they got was higher taxes. In the end it cost him his throne. In 1658, Aurangzeb, his third son with Mumtaz Mahal, deposed the ailing Shah, locking him in a tower of the Red Fort, where he would spend his last days gazing out at his masterpiece. On his death in 1666, he was entombed inside the Taj Mahal beside his lover for all eternity.

The cost may have been high, but the result is exquisite. The entire building is made of glistening white marble. At its core is a central dome shaped like an enormous pearl, 240 feet high, surrounded by four smaller domes, each one framed by 130-foot minarets. The entire building is encircled by a 100-foot red sandstone wall, which opens to an enormous reflecting pool and a lush garden laid out

Photo: Dan Searle

before the temple in perfect symmetry. Waterways divide the beds of cypress and fruit trees into quarters, symbolising the Islamic Gardens of Paradise, whose four rivers run with water, milk, wine and honey. In mist it appears to float above the ground. Its colours change with the arc of the day: soft pink at dawn, dazzling white and then golden when lit by the glow of a full moon. The poet Rabindranath Tagore called it 'a teardrop on the cheek of eternity', and so far he's been proved right. Here, all strands of the Mughal aesthetic histories – Islamic, Persian and Indian – are woven together into one perfect manifestation of architectural beauty.

But the true marvel of the Taj Mahal is that its grandeur is somehow matched by the intricateness of its detail. The walls are decorated with carved floral bouquets, each inlaid with precious stones from across the globe: jade, turquoise, lapis lazuli and coral. Subtle shades of marble, sandstone and slate interweave the building like delicate threads of silk. Beside the tomb itself, a 186-foot square block of marble set in an octagonal chamber, the memorial to the Shah and his Queen is so elaborate that each single adorning leaf is composed of dozens of uniquely fashioned, individual precious stones. There is calligraphy throughout. Verses from the Quran are inscribed along the arched entrances, inlaid with black marble, the typography increasing in dimension the higher one looks, creating the illusion that the lettering is the same size throughout. And there, in the centre of it all, the words, as if spoken by the Shah himself: 'Help us oh lord to bear what we cannot bear' – his immortal testament to the enduring power of love, and the agony of its final departure.

WHERE: Agra, India (Uttar Pradesh).

HOW TO SEE IT: Agra is approximately two hours from

Delhi by train. The Taj Mahal is open sunrise to sunset, but closed on Fridays to accommodate Muslims wishing to pray there. The weather is coolest November through January, which means it's also the peak season. Summer temperatures can reach 50°C. Time your visit with a full moon. Night-time tickets are sold five days a month to coincide with the lunar cycle or simply book a room with a view from one of the many nearby hotels.

www.tajmahal.gov.in

TOP TIPS: Arrive at dawn and run to the cenotaph chamber, literally. If you can get there first, before the noise of the crowd, you will hear what is described as 'the sound of infinity' – a subtle vibration created by air moving through the huge dome.

TRY THIS INSTEAD: Humayun's tomb in the Nizamuddin area of Delhi may not quite match the splendour of the Taj Mahal, but there are fewer crowds and the sublime symmetry of the Mughal architecture is still awe-inspiring. Also, don't miss Agra's other attractions, including the Red Fort where Shah Jahan spent his final days.

www.incredibleindia.org

KUMBH MELA, INDIA

The Hindu Kumbh Mela festival in India is the largest act of faith on the planet. In recent years more than 100 million people have taken part in the 55-day event – more than the entire population of the United Kingdom. If held in

Photo: Lokankara

Madison Square Garden in New York City, it would sell out for more than 5,000 consecutive nights, or roughly fifteen years. Taking all personal histories and beliefs aside, it is, without a doubt, the most significant single religious event on Earth and the largest gathering of people on the planet.

The festival is held every three years, alternating between four pilgrimage sites located on four sacred rivers: the Ganges at Haridwar, the Shipra at Ujjain, the Godavari at Nashik, and on the confluence of the Ganges and the Yamuna at Allahabad, the largest and most auspicious. No one knows exactly when it began. There are travellers' accounts from at least the 7th century, and it has been recorded in Hindu texts for thousands of years, but the legends also speak of a much earlier creation.

At the time when the universe was being formed, they say, the Indian Devas, a kind of demigod, lost all their powers as a result of a curse. Lord Vishnu, the preserver of the universe in Hindu beliefs, told them to fetch a pot filled with the nectar of immortality and churn it in the Ksheer Sagar, the divine ocean. But they couldn't manage it alone and so asked the demons for help. Together they worked at it for thousands of years. But when the nectar finally arose from the sea, the gods feared the demons would drink it and become immortal themselves. A fierce battle broke out, during which Garuda, a celestial bird and the vehicle of Vishnu, flew away with the nectar. But as she did, four drops spilt on four places of the Earth and it is those places where the Kumbh, which means 'pot' in Sanskrit, is held.

The central focus of the festival is the river. Devotees believe that by bathing in the sacred waters at this holy time, in the exact spot where the nectar fell, they will be cleansed of their sins and freed from the cycle of rebirth and death. It begins with a procession, led by the *sadhus*, the holy men. First the Nagas, naked and covered in ash with long matted hair and bloodshot eyes, then the emaciated bodies of the Urdhwavahurs, withered from ascetic spiritual practices, followed by the Parivajakas, who have taken a vow of silence and the Shirshasins, who remain standing their whole lives. All the holy men of India, covered in garlands and chanting 'har har gangey', long live Ganges, as they immerse themselves in the holy river. Behind them are women in colourful saris, men stripped to their underwear and children, all of them jumping into the icy water, hundreds of thousands at a time, with millions more on the banks beside them. In the evening, yogis, sages and mystics recount stories and read from sacred texts; bands play, people dance, there is rejoicing everywhere. The Kumbh Mela is a spectacle of faith, colour and raw humanity unrivalled anywhere on the planet.

But it is more than that too. A sense of the divine, whatever that may be, is one of the cornerstones of our very existence. The Kumbh Mela is the largest religious event on the planet, but it's also the ultimate manifestation of belief itself and a symbol of what it means to be human.

WHERE: Allahabad, Haridwar, Nashik and Ujjain, India (rotating every three years).

HOW TO SEE IT: All are welcome, foreigners and non-Hindus alike. Dates vary widely according to astrological predictions.
www.kumbhmela.net

TOP TIP: Beware of bathing in rivers, they are notoriously polluted.

TRY THIS INSTEAD: Holi festival is the Hindu festival of colour, held throughout India the day after the full moon in March each year. People throw coloured powder over each other, smear themselves in paint, dance and have parties all day. In Mathura, four hours from Delhi, celebrations can last for sixteen days.
www.incredibleindia.org

THE FORBIDDEN CITY, CHINA

The Forbidden City in Beijing is the largest palace complex in the world. More than 3,000 feet long, 2,400 feet across and ringed by a moat 170 feet wide, it covers a total area of 2.3 million square feet. There are 980 buildings and nearly 10,000 rooms inside. Treasures adorn every wall. For 500 years, from 1420 to 1911, 24 successive Chinese emperors ruled their kingdom from within this complex. But the Forbidden City was more than just an imperial residence. For the ancient Chinese, this was the centre of their entire universe. The emperor was a direct link between the earthly world of his subjects and the ethereal abode of the gods. For them, this truly was heaven on earth.

Construction began in 1406, under the orders of Zhu Di, third emperor of the Ming dynasty, after he decided to move the capital from Nanjing to his power base in Beijing, more than 600 miles to the north. Such a move was considered a travesty to ancestral law, so to appease the gods, and the officials of his court, he built his new imperial palace according to the ancient ordering principles of feng shui, ensuring the new capital would be enshrined in positive energy.

As such, all buildings face south to honour the sun and ward against evil, cold spirits from the north. The layout is then arranged around a north–south axis, based on a diagram of the ancient Chinese vision of the cosmic universe, and aligned with the pole star, which emphasises the emperor's central position as the son of heaven. Everything to the left, the east, is yang, the masculine, where the sun rises. Everything to the right, the west, is yin, the feminine, where the sun sets. There is a compositional balance across these divides too: buildings, courtyards and open space complement each other in perfect symmetry. Even the site itself, surrounded by the water of the moat, and Jingshan mountain to the north, can be seen to adhere to these principles of balance and accord.

The layout also adheres to the strict Confucian principles of hierarchy, demanded of Chinese society at the time. The palaces and major halls are located on central axes. Minor buildings, for lesser dignitaries, would fall in parallel to either side. The southern half of the city, the outer court as it is known, was the public domain, where the emperor would host dignitaries and conduct state business and religious ceremonies. The inner court, in the northern half, was his private realm, the residence of his family, wives and concubines, of which there were thousands. No other men were allowed here after dark, save for his army of male servants, eunuchs every one. There could be no risk of infidelity at the emperor's palace.

But few would ever see it because 32-foot walls prevented anyone from looking in and those who arrived uninvited would pay for it with their life. It was called the Forbidden City precisely because entrance was prohibited to all but a handful of family, court officials and servants. But those who did saw an almost unimaginable splendour.

Photo: Daniel Case

The buildings are bold red, made of precious *Phoebe zhennan* wood, with yellow tiled roofs, arcing upwards like the edge of a smile. Enormous marble courtyards, capable of holding 100,000, are flanked by three Grand Halls, each one raised up on a three-tier marble terrace and surrounded by towering balustrades. The most important, the 115-foot tall Hall of Supreme Harmony, is the largest timber structure in the country, framed by golden tiles and two eleven-foot dragon statues, the symbol of the emperor. And in its centre is the Dragon Throne itself, carved of nanmu, sandalwood and gold on a seven-stepped platform adorned in pearls and thirteen carvings of dragons within. It was from here that the emperor would rule with supreme authority. The entire court would have to touch their forehead on the ground nine times, a practice known as kowtowing, in his presence.

Further inside there are huge stone reliefs, carved with mythical creatures, a 250-tonne marble carriageway, adorned with dragons and clouds, palaces and temples stretching beyond the horizon, screens of silk and bells of gold. It is, without a doubt, the greatest work of Chinese architecture the world has ever seen. Their culture and cosmology are embedded in every stone. The last emperor, Puyi, abdicated in 1912 at just six years old. With him went centuries of history and culture, the pinnacle of one of the world's great ancient civilisations. Those days may be gone, but to be here is to feel that forbidden world come alive once again.

WHERE: Beijing, China.

HOW TO SEE IT: Allow at least a half day to see the whole thing. Avoid weekends and Chinese holidays, when the hordes of tourists are so thick it's almost impossible to see

many of the main attractions. Closed on Mondays.
http://english.visitbeijing.com.cn

TOP TIP: The best view of the Forbidden City as a whole is from the top of Coal Hill in Jingshan Park.

TRY THIS INSTEAD: The spectacular Potala Palace in Lhasa, Tibet, was once the seat of Tibetan government and winter residence of the Dalai Lamas. A magnificent symbol of this unique and fascinating country.
www.dalailama.com

SON DOONG CAVE, VIETNAM

Deep in the jungles of Phong Nha-Ke Bang National Park in the Quang Binh province of Vietnam, a local farmer, Ho Khanh, was sheltering from a storm. He had been searching for rare wood in the forests around his home when the heavy rains forced him to take refuge at the base of a cliff. Looking down, he noticed a dark hole in the ground. He could feel a huge wind rushing up from beneath him and the distant sound of a fast flowing river far below. He didn't know it at the time, and it would be twenty years before he would return, but Ho Kanh had just discovered the largest cave in the world.

That was in 1991. In 2009, a team of British explorers, led by Howard Limbert, heard rumour of Ho Khanh's story. They had spent the best part of six years searching this dense and near impenetrable jungle for possible caves. The entire national park is situated above a huge limestone

massif, which has been hollowed out over the centuries by intense rainfall, resulting in the formation of hundreds of underground caverns. Somewhere beneath them they knew a truly enormous cave must be waiting to be found. Ho Khanh took them to it.

Hang Son Doong, which means 'mountain river cave', is more than 600 feet high and 300 feet wide. The largest chamber extends continuously for 2.5 miles, but the cave itself stretches on for another three. Inside are chambers that could fit a New York City block, with skyscrapers 40 stories tall. A Boeing 747 could fly through and not scratch its wings. The cave is so big, in fact, that it has its own weather system inside. Clouds linger around two enormous collapsed roofs, natural skylights 300 feet across. Where the light shines, forest grows: a subterranean jungle, 600 feet underground, with hanging vines, rare plants, milky white insects and a troop of monkeys – probably the only ones in the world to make their home beneath the earth. It's like entering a lost world. Gargantuan stalactites hang from the ceiling like giant's candle wax; 250-foot stalagmites sprout up from the ground like enormous alien sculptures. There are cave pearls as big as baseballs. And through it all, the river, a raging torrent that is still scouring Son Doong deeper each year.

That first expedition struggled their way through the darkness for five days, but were stopped before they could complete their mission. An enormous calcite barrier, more than 200 feet high, jokingly referred to as 'The Great Wall of Vietnam', blocked their path. The next year they returned with the right equipment and painstakingly scaled it. At the top there was a glimmer of daylight. They had reached the end of Son Doong and mapped the largest cave on the planet. Here was a place untouched for at least 2 million years, a portal in time. And it's not alone. Somewhere beneath these tropical forests are more giant caves, of that Limbert and his team are sure. Who knows: perhaps one is even bigger, its secrets still waiting to be discovered.

WHERE: Phong Nha-Ke Bang National Park, Vietnam.

HOW TO SEE IT: At the time of writing, there was only one licensed tour operator allowed to offer trips inside Son Doong. Oxalis has a five-day trip, which includes three days exploring and two nights camping out inside Son Doong cave.
www.oxalis.com.vn
www.sondoongcave.org

TOP TIP: Make sure you have a good level of fitness before undertaking this trip. There is a six-hour jungle trek just to reach the cave and then multiple river crossings, abseils and rock scrambles within.

TRY THIS INSTEAD: Deciding what is the biggest cave in the world is no easy feat. Deer Cave in Malaysia has a single chamber that is probably bigger but definitely not as long. While the cave system in Mammoth National Park, Kentucky, is far longer, stretching more than 400 miles underground, no individual cavern is anywhere near as big within it. Hang Son Doong is therefore widely considered the largest single cave in the world. But the other two would make great alternatives for an adventurous trip.
www.mulunationalpark.com
www.nps.gov/maca

ANGKOR WAT, CAMBODIA

Angkor Wat is the largest religious structure ever built. Created more than 2,000 years ago, deep in the jungles of Cambodia, four miles north of Siem Reap, the five towers of this enormous temple rise 700 feet above the canopy, like giant lotus buds carved in stone. The outer balustrade is 3,000 feet long, the moat three miles across and 650 feet wide. The entire site covers 500 acres, roughly the size of the entire principality of Monaco, and is filled with enormous galleries, courtyards, pools and chambers throughout.

But it is not alone. Angkor Wat is only a small part of a much larger network of temples that make up the Angkor Archaeological Park. This 1,000-year-old ruined compound was once the capital city of the mighty Khmer empire, which thrived here between the 9th and 15th centuries and controlled vast swathes of South-east Asia, from Cambodia through much of Thailand, Vietnam and Laos. In total, the park covers an area of more than 150 square miles, more than six times the size of Manhattan, making it easily the largest metropolis ever constructed in the pre-industrial world. At its peak, 1 million people lived here.

And it may have been even larger than first thought. Recent laser analysis of the surrounding jungle floor has revealed a series of previously undiscovered medieval cities, between 900 and 1,400 years old, buried under the dense tropical undergrowth. Interwoven between these are the remnants of ancient canals, a road network and complex water and irrigation systems. Taken together, this sophisticated network of cities would have rivalled even Cambodia's modern capital Phnom Penh in scope today.

They built many spectacular temples here: the huge stone faces of Bayon, the jungle vines slowly strangling the ruins of Ta Prohm. But Angkor Wat is special. It was constructed, in part, to be the mausoleum of its king, Suryavarman II, but also as a homage to the Hindu god Vishnu, whose ten-foot tall statue marks the western entrance. Indeed, Hindu cosmology forms the basis of the entire architecture. The moat is symbolic of the Hindu Cosmic Sea, source of life and creative energy. The walled enclosures represent holy mountains, obstacles that must be overcome on the path to enlightenment. The central tower is Mount Meru, the mythical Hindu abode of the gods. Each successive area becomes more sacred as it becomes more removed from the outside world.

The immensity of Angkor Wat is matched only by the exquisiteness of its detail. A half-mile bas-relief wraps around the central temple depicting tales from Khmer history and recreations of sacred texts, including an enormous 150-foot portrayal of the 'churning of the sea of milk', a Hindu creation story in which the gods attempt to stir the elixir of immortality out of the milk of time. Pillars are sculpted with lotus rosettes, walls with dancing animals, there are sculptures of serpents and gods throughout. But perhaps most beguiling of all are the more than 3,000 apsaras, heavenly nymphs, hidden within the grounds, each one individually carved with unique hair, clothes and floral tributes. Everywhere one looks there is artistry and finesse.

But it wasn't easy: 300,000 workers and 6,000 elephants spent 30 years on the task. To create the moat alone, 53 million cubic feet of sand and silt had to be removed. Then, a 21-mile canal had to be dug through the dense jungle in order to transport 10 million bricks, including enormous sandstone blocks, weighing more than 3,000 pounds, from quarries 30 miles away.

Photo: Rémi Jouan

But then having invested this enormous effort, they suddenly left. One of the great mysteries of archaeology has been why, in the 15th century when the Khmer empire was at the peak of its prosperity and power, they suddenly abandoned their crown jewel and resettled in Phnom Penh instead. One answer may be water. The Khmer were masters of irrigation, producing an enormous network of channels, levees and reservoirs that allowed them to harness the seasonal rains and provide fresh drinking water and irrigate crops for their vast population. That system may have failed. Changing climate could have brought more intense periods of rain and drought. As the population grew, increasing deforestation could have heralded floods, bringing sediment into the water and causing irrecoverable damage to the entire system. The Khmer may have abandoned Angkor because they simply became too numerous to survive here.

But the glory of Angkor Wat is undiminished by its demise. It is a masterpiece of Khmer architecture and the pinnacle of their once formidable empire. Not only the largest religious structure in the world, but perhaps the most intricate and awe-inspiring too.

WHERE: Angkor Archaeological Park, Siem Reap, Cambodia.

HOW TO SEE IT: Siem Reap is the best base for exploring the temples, with a wide selection of hotels, restaurants and amenities to suit all budgets. As Angkor Wat is still considered a sacred site to the Khmer people, it is important to dress sensitively: shirts must cover upper arms and shorts must go to the knees. Avoid the monsoon in May–June.
www.tourismcambodia.com

TOP TIP: Go to Phnom Bakheng temple for the best sunsets and Angkor Wat for the best sunrise.

TRY THIS INSTEAD: Bagan in central Myanmar is a spectacular complex of more than 2,000 temples, with far fewer visitors than Angkor Wat.
www.myanmar.travel

TERRACOTTA ARMY, CHINA

In March 1974, a group of farmers digging a well outside the city of Xi'an in China struck upon a fragment of an old figurine. Archaeologists were called in and gradually a life-size clay soldier, sword in hand, as if poised for battle, was found buried whole in the earth. And he was not alone. Those farmers had accidently broken through to an underground pit containing a total of 6,000 life-size statues. This was the terracotta army of Qin Shi Huang, the first emperor of China, who lived over 2,200 years ago. They are the guardians of his tomb and their discovery is one of the greatest archaeological finds of the 20th century.

Qin Shi Huangdi rose to power in 246 BC, at the age of thirteen, and by 221 BC he had unified the region's warring kingdoms and declared himself the first emperor of all China. During his reign he achieved many things: standardising weights and measures, introducing a unified writing script, advancing agricultural infrastructure across the country and building the first incarnation of the Great Wall of China, which would hold for more than 1,000 years until the Ming dynasty expanded and improved upon his concept. He was also obsessed with the idea of immortality,

Photo: David Castor

chasing fantastical elixirs across the known world. Ironically, it was during one such quest that he died, searching for herbs his alchemists said would prolong his life. But in a strange way his dream has finally come true. Qin Shi Huangdi's mausoleum took 37 years and more than 700,000 people to complete. But it still stands today. His terracotta army was built to accompany him to the afterlife – warriors to rule the heavens with – and it is they who have now resurrected his memory from the grave for all to see.

The scale of what he created is formidable. In that first pit alone, 756 feet long, 200 feet wide and nearly 50 feet deep, there stands row upon row of life-size warriors, shoulder to shoulder, as if standing to attention. Lines of foot soldiers, archers, cavalry riders, horses and war chariots arranged into battle formation ready to strike; 1,000 have been unearthed, but there are an estimated 5,000 more still underground. An entire brigade of ancient Chinese troops made entirely of clay. And they are all unique: 3D facial analysis has revealed that no two terracotta soldiers are the same, each one modelled, it is believed, after the real fighters of the time.

And the detail is staggering. Rivets of body armour are embossed in perfect detail; the tread from the soles of shoes can be seen; we can make out individual lines of hair, beards, the unique curvature of hands and eyes. They have faded now, but in places a trace of paint remains, hinting that at the time of their creation their battle robes would have glistened with striking hues of red, green and jet black. Beside them are real weapons too: bronze swords, quivers of 100 arrows sharpened to a point, crossbows, spears.

And this is just one pit. Three more neighbouring pits have since been unearthed revealing crossbowmen, officers, generals, acrobats, scribes. Not just an army, but a civil service and entertainment too. To date, the remains of nearly 8,000 terracotta figures have been recovered, each one moulded and painstakingly carved by hand. But it is estimated that many thousands more remain buried underground. Archaeologists have now identified an enormous complex of subterranean vaults surrounding his tomb, some 600 pits, spread out over a 22-square-mile radius.

And the greatest treasures may still remain to be found. Accounts from the time indicate that Qin Shi Huang's tomb was filled with scaled down replicas of his palace, pavilions and offices; there were miniature mountains made of bronze, precious stones for the sun and stars, and rivers flowing with mercury to the sea. But, for now, his secrets will remain buried with him. Archaeologists fear any excavation may irrecoverably damage whatever treasures lie within. The terracotta warriors, it seems, have done their job, protecting his body and preserving his memory for all time.

WHERE: Xi'an, China.

HOW TO SEE IT: The Museum of Qin Terra Cotta Warriors and Horses is about an hour's bus ride from Xi'an train station. The exhibition features access to the original dig site as well as other displays and information. But consider a few days to see the surrounding region as well. Xi'an is regarded as one of China's most pleasant cities, with 40-foot-high ancient walls and the towering Mount Huashan nearby, one of the country's five holy Taoist peaks. www.cnto.org

TOP TIPS: Hire a guide: there is very little English signage and the audio-guide is hard to understand. Group or private tours can be booked from Xi'an in advance or there are usually guides available on site. Avoid national holidays and peak hours to beat the crowds, start early or aim for around noon when the coach trips break for lunch.

TRY THIS INSTEAD: It's not quite the real thing, but the Terracotta Warriors Museum in Dorset, England, is one of the few museums outside of China dedicated exclusively to the Terracotta Warriors. All the displays are replicas, which have been specially made by the technicians of the Lintong Museum Cultural Relic Workshop, Xi'an, China, as well as workshops of the China National Arts & Crafts Corporation, Xi'an. www.terracottawarriors.co.uk

OCEANIA

ULURU, AUSTRALIA

Uluru, or Ayers Rock, is an enormous sandstone monolith deep in the Northern Territory of central Australia. At 1,142 feet tall, 5.8 miles around and extending more than 1.5 miles under the earth, Ernest Giles, the first European to discover it, called it 'the remarkable pebble'. And so it is. A single block of rock, taller than the Eiffel Tower in Paris or the Chrysler Building in New York City, rising suddenly from the surrounding desert plain as if placed there by supernatural powers.

And it may well have been. No other place in the country is so rich in Aboriginal mythology and so soaked in spiritual significance. Aborigines are the oldest living culture on Earth. They have been walking these lands for at least 30,000 years, maybe more, and Uluru is their most hallowed ground.

Geologists will tell you it's the remnants of a vast sedimentary seabed dried out, raised, folded and eroded by the movement of the Earth's crust. The Aborigines have a different story. There is evidence of continuous habitation in this area for at least the last 10,000 years. The Pitjantjatjara, Yankunytjatjara and Anangu tribes, who still live here, are the direct descendants of those people. For them, Uluru was formed in the dreamtime – the period of creation itself, when ancestral beings rose up from the featureless void, took form and manifested the physical world we see today. As these spirits became animals, humans and birds, they travelled the Earth, creating mountains, rivers, deserts and trees through their actions. Evidence of their passage can still be seen throughout the landscape: the deep ridges on the side of Uluru were the tracks made by the carpet-snake people as they went to and from the water-hole; small depressions on the summit are where they rested.

Once they had created the world, the ancestral beings transformed into it: they became rocks, stars and watering holes. These locations today are imbued with spiritual power. Especially at Uluru, whose many caves and fissures are covered in petroglyphs that testify to this fact.

But for the Aborigines, these sacred spots are not just representations of their ancestral beings, they are actually their ancestral beings; they exist for real in those forms today. Saying that boulder is the petrified body of a spiritual being is not meant as a metaphor; it is literally the body of a fallen being, immortalised in stone. In this way, by coming into contact with these sacred spots, by touching the face of Uluru, they can touch the dreamtime itself.

The Aboriginal culture of Australia is unique because there is still a direct line to the past today. In other cultures

Photo: Corey Leopold

we may hazard guesses at the meanings of ancient rock art or how our stone-age ancestors once lived, thought and believed, but here we need only ask. The stories, dances and songs they sing today are the same ones passed down, from generation to generation, from time immemorial. In their belief, all that is sacred is in the land. The land itself is spirit, not in metaphor or myth, but an actual, essential component of the soul itself. They are the Earth and the Earth is them.

In many ways, so are we all. Our bodies are made of the same stuff as rocks and trees and dirt. And to them we will one day return. Perhaps that's the true wonder of Uluru: the oldest living culture in the world, still thriving and keeping its traditions alive, speaking through mountains, and monoliths of stone, that there is no division between Earth, body and spirit. That it is all one thing.

WHERE: Uluru-Kata Tjuta National Park, Australia.

HOW TO SEE IT: The nearest town is Yulara, 290 miles south-west of Alice Springs in the Northern Territory. It's also possible to fly directly to Ayers Rock Airport, twenty miles away, directly from Sydney and Cairns. Visit the Uluru-Kata Tjuta Aboriginal Cultural Centre nearby to find out more about the indigenous culture of the region. www.parksaustralia.gov.au/uluru

TOP TIPS: Come at sunrise and sunset for the most spectacular view, when the rock glows bright orange and red. For the best experience, hire a local Aboriginal guide.

TRY THIS INSTEAD: Kata Tjuta is another sacred Aboriginal rock formation twenty miles away. Make sure to see both on your trip.

THE GREAT BARRIER REEF, AUSTRALIA

The Great Barrier Reef is the largest reef system in the world. Covering an area of 135,000 square miles, it is bigger than the United Kingdom, Holland and Switzerland combined. It stretches for more than 1,400 miles along the Queensland coast, from the northern tip of Cape York to south of Bundaberg. Lay it out across Europe and it would reach from London to Moscow, making it the largest living structure on the planet and the only one visible from outer space.

It's ancient too. Generation after generation of coral has grown on top of its predecessors, creating an enormous underwater wall of stone, more than 150 miles wide at points, along Australia's north-eastern shore. The thin layer of living coral on its tip is at least 6,000 years old, comprised of the largest collection of coral species on the planet: more than 400 separate hard and soft varieties – one-third of the world's total. But while most reefs alive today are estimated to be less than 10,000 years old in total, the Great Barrier Reef began forming a staggering 18 million years ago, when megalodons still prowled the sea.

But it's not a single entity, rather it's comprised of a network of thousands of individual coral reefs, tropical islands, cays and mangrove isles. Together they form one of the most biologically diverse places on the planet. Under these waves are more than 11,000 individual species: 1,500 types of fish (roughly 10 per cent of the world's total), 30 varieties of whales and dolphins, more than 100 types of sharks and rays, six species of sea turtle, 100 jellyfish, 4,000 molluscs as well as sea crocodiles, dugongs, starfish and more.

The effect is dazzling: layer upon layer of kaleidoscopic submarine gardens adorned with orange fire tubes, pink

Photo: Toby Hudson

brains, bright yellow mushrooms and purple and green sea-thread swaying in the current like leaves in a storm. Rainbows of Angel Fish, Damselfish and spotted red Coral Trout weave in and out of the living architecture. Enormous schools of shining silver shimmer like comets in the refracted sun. From the air it appears like an abstract painting, patterns of deep blue framed in pure turquoise and lined with windswept waves. Under the water, there is almost unimaginable colour and beauty.

But the entire ecosystem is in danger. Chemical run off from farms and industry, as well as over fishing, has always been a constant threat. But now climate change is taking the greatest toll. Warmer ocean temperatures put stress on the coral reefs and lead to coral bleaching, the point at which they expel the tiny algae that live inside their tissue and provide them with food and colour. If the stress continues, the coral will die. On top of this are the effects of carbon dioxide on seawater. The ocean is one of the biggest absorbers of CO_2 emissions on the planet, helping to soak up roughly half of what humans produce. But that process makes the ocean more acidic, which weakens the coral. Since the industrial age CO_2 levels have risen 40 per cent, from 280 parts per million (ppm) to roughly 385 ppm today. At 400 ppm the ocean's coral will begin to break down. By 500 ppm it will be extinct. And if the coral reefs collapse the entire food chain may collapse with it.

But there is still hope. The Great Barrier Reef is a true phenomenon of the natural world, a spectacular undersea universe that is as enormous as it is ancient. Its future may be in precarious balance, but the inspiration to fight for it is clear for all who put on a mask and look under the waves to see.

WHERE: Queensland, Australia.

HOW TO SEE IT: There are almost limitless ways of experiencing the Great Barrier Reef, from snorkelling and scuba-diving to helicopter and submarine rides. Most day trips leave from major coastal centres like Cairns and Port Douglas. Or try a multi-day cruise or overnight stay on one of its many islands. It's possible to visit the Great Barrier Reef year round; peak season is the Australian summer, December to March, and also the wettest. The southern winter, June to August, offers milder temperatures and less rain. www.greatbarrierreef.org

TOP TIP: To capture the best underwater photographs, use a red filter. Water naturally filters out the colour red from sunlight, so in order to recreate the most vibrant images you need to manually add it in.

TRY THIS INSTEAD: The second largest barrier reef in the world is the Belize Reef, at 190 miles long. See it off the Caribbean coast of Belize. http://travelbelize.com

MOAI STATUES, RAPA NUI

The island of Rapa Nui is one of the most remote places on the planet. Located 2,300 miles off the west coast of South America, Easter Island, as it's also known, is 1,000 miles from its nearest neighbour: a speck of land, fourteen miles long and seven miles across, in the middle of the South Pacific Sea. For the small group of Polynesians who somehow managed to row here more than 800 years ago, crossing the vastness of the wild and uncharted ocean in nothing but simple wooden canoes, it became known as Te Pito o Te Henua, 'the navel of the world'. This was the centre of their entire universe. Nothing existed but this sliver of rock and the infinite horizon of the sea. Yet, somehow, they blossomed here, developing advanced agriculture, music, art and the only written script of the time ever found in the region – a kind of hieroglyphics called Rongorongo, which is still being deciphered today. But what they are famous for are the moai: 887 monolithic statues placed, as if standing watch, on the edge of the sea. To this day no one knows exactly why they were built or how they got there.

The original inhabitants arrived sometime around AD 1200. They began carving the moai almost immediately and continued near continuously until the first European contact in 1722, with a group of Dutch explorers. It was an enormous undertaking. Using only stone chisels, called *toki*, each of these giant head and torso sculptures, up to 40 feet tall and 75 tonnes in weight, were quarried from the base of the Rano Raraku volcano out of tuff, a rock formed from compressed volcanic ash. They then had to be transported across the island and placed on top of *ahu* bases, a kind of ceremonial platform, eventually forming a ring around the coastline. There, at their final resting place, eye sockets were carved into the statues, with irises of coral and pupils of obsidian, marking them now as a 'living face'. Their expressions are long and sombre, with straight mouths and a sharp hawk-like nose. Most people know them as disembodied heads, but many have bodies too, covered on the back in strange markings, like ancient tattoos.

They were most likely built to honour important members of the tribe after they had passed away. Despite being placed on the edge of the coast, each statue actually looks inwards, back at the island, as if the spirits of these former chieftains are still watching over the populace.

But how they managed to move them is still a matter of debate. Many broken statues are scattered throughout the island, showing they were probably transported upright and would occasionally fall and smash en route. Indeed, only 32 per cent of the total moai ever created made it to their final destination. For years it was thought a system of rollers was used, involving lumber from around the island. But Rapa Nui legends speak of the statues walking to their ceremonial platforms themselves. A recent theory has shown that by tying ropes around a statue, they can be rocked from side to side while being simultaneously pulled from the front, creating a kind of walking motion that slowly inches them forward. The legends, it may turn out, were right all along.

Whatever their true purpose, or how they arrived, the people who built them vanished soon after contact with the outside world, ravaged by disease and the devastating effects of deforestation. But a few descendants remain and they are still guarded over by the moai to this day. The word 'moai' means 'so that he can exist'. Their hope, in building them, may have been to grant some kind of eternal life, to mark in stone the lives of those who once lived, to beat death. The people of Rapa Nui lived in one of the remotest parts of the planet, but the legend of what they built has somehow travelled across the globe. In many ways, their wish, the enduring purpose of the moai, has come true.

WHERE: Rapa Nui (Easter Island), Chile.

HOW TO SEE IT: Flights depart from Santiago, Chile, and Tahiti. High season is January to March, the southern hemisphere summer, but the weather is fairly pleasant

Photo: Aurbina

year round. Cars, motorcycles and mountain bikes are available to hire and a good way to explore the island's many archaeological sites. There are also great beaches, diving and surfing.
www.chile.travel/en

TOP TIP: The best sites for photographs are Ahu Tongariki, where fifteen well-preserved moai stand looking towards the hills, and the quarry of Rano Raraku, where there are numerous half-finished sculptures.

TRY THIS INSTEAD: For a mysterious monolith that's closer to home, try the Scottish standing stones. Although not carved in the same way as the moai, they share much of the mystery about why they were created and how they were transported to their final sites. Some of the most famous, and spectacular, are the Callanish Stones on the Isle of Lewis.
www.callanishvisitorcentre.co.uk

THE MARIANA TRENCH, PACIFIC OCEAN

The Mariana Trench is the deepest part of the world's oceans. Its lowest point, known as the Challenger Deep, is 36,070 feet beneath the surface – deeper than the cruising height of a commercial airliner. If Mount Everest were placed inside, its summit would still be more than a mile under the sea. And thousands of climbers have scaled to the top of that peak. Only three have ever ventured to these depths. We know more about the surface of Mars than we do about the deepest parts of our own ocean. It is truly the last frontier on

Earth. And its secrets may one day teach us about the origins of life itself.

Located in the western Pacific, 124 miles east of Guam and the Mariana Islands, the Mariana Trench is a 1,500-mile long, 43-mile wide crescent-shaped scar on the ocean floor, more than five times the size of the Grand Canyon. It is an alien place. No light can reach its depths. The pressure is 1,000 times greater than at the surface. Temperatures are barely above freezing. There are pools of liquid sulphur and hydrothermal vents that erupt at 450°C. And yet, somehow, life exists: fantastical creatures glow with bright luminescence – an entire universe hidden in the darkness, deep beneath the waves.

The first people to set eyes on it were Jacques Piccard and Navy Lt Don Walsh, in 1960, on board a US Navy submersible, called the *Trieste*. The pair descended for five hours and spent twenty minutes at the very bottom of the world. But it would be more than 50 years before their feat was repeated. On 26 March 2012, James Cameron, the Hollywood director more famous for films such as *Avatar* and (ironically) *Titanic*, successfully piloted a specially constructed submersible, called *Deepsea Challenger*, which he himself helped design, all the way to the bottom of the Mariana Trench. The expedition was fraught with danger. There was only enough room for him to travel alone, cramped into a tiny sphere too small to move more than a few inches. At those depths the ship could implode like a crumpled tin can, the windows could crack and the sea could pour in, he could lose communication and be set adrift, or freeze.

But he didn't. Cameron descended 6.77 miles to the seabed, collected samples and filmed the entire thing in stunning 3D. He described it as desolate and bleak, utterly cut off from the world. But also a place where there is beauty,

where 'you feel the power of nature's imagination, which is so much greater than our own'. The science from that first expedition is still being unravelled. But what is for sure is that there is life even there. He found giant amphipods, prawn-like crustaceans, sea cucumbers, microbial mats and enormous single-cell xenophyophores – all of which have never been seen before.

The potential ramifications of these finds are enormous. Many microorganisms discovered in the deep ocean are already being used to develop new medicines for cancer, Alzheimer's and more. The possibilities for biotech are even greater: one finding from this first mission suggests that the cells discovered on microbial mats at the bottom of the ocean may help regulate the amount of CO_2 in the environment and lessen the effects of global warming. We may learn about our origins down there too. Scientists believe that it was in trenches exactly like the Mariana where the precise conditions of life may have first sprung. And if it worked here, perhaps it will work elsewhere. By searching the alien world at the bottom of our sea, we may learn to detect the first alien worlds in the far reaches of space too.

We live on an ocean planet: 70 per cent of the Earth's surface area is covered by water. And yet, less than 5 per cent of our oceans have been explored. The maps we have of the sea floor are less detailed than the maps we have of the moon, Mars or Venus. James Cameron will be going down again soon. And it's lucky he is. Who knows what secrets are waiting for him at the very bottom of the world?

WHERE: Mariana Trench Marine National Monument, Pacific Ocean.

HOW TO SEE IT: Find out where to watch the 3D film

of James Cameron's expedition at his website: www. deepseachallenge.com

TOP TIP: Keep your eye on the National Oceanic and Atmospheric Administration's website for links to live video feeds from their deep-water explorations.
www.noaa.gov

TRY THIS INSTEAD: Visit the *Titanic* wreck, 12,500 feet below the surface of the North Atlantic Ocean on a Russian Mir submersible kitted out for tourists. But it's not cheap: expect to pay $30,000 or more for the privilege.
www.thebluefish.com/visit-the-titanic

ARCTIC/ANTARCTICA

THE LAMBERT GLACIER, ANTARCTICA

The Lambert Glacier in Antarctica is the largest glacier in the world: 270 miles long, up to 60 miles wide and more than 8,000 feet deep, it drains 8 per cent of the total Antarctic ice sheet and is one of the fastest moving ice streams on the planet. At its peak, velocities reach more than 3,000 feet each year – a genuine river of ice, flowing from the depths of the continent into the Amery ice shelf and the sea. There, at its final destination, one of the rarest and most beautiful sights in the polar world is found: jade-green icebergs, formed by high levels of mineral content trapped inside the ice.

But the Lambert Glacier is only one spectacle in a land

of superlatives. Antarctica is truly a wonder in itself. It is both the largest desert on the planet and the largest single mass of ice, the Antarctic Ice Sheet, covering an area over 5 million square miles, almost double the size of the USA. In places, the ice is over 15,000 feet thick, more than five times as deep as the world's tallest building is high. Entire mountain ranges, lakes and volcanoes are buried beneath its frozen mass. The coldest temperature ever recorded was found here: −93.2°C − closer to the surface temperature of Mars than anywhere else on Earth. Icebergs as big as cities regularly snap off and float to sea. The largest ever seen was 170 miles long and 25 miles wide − nearly seven times the size of London.

It may be one of the most inhospitable places on Earth, but some of the world's greatest wildlife spectacles are, nevertheless, found here: killer whales, elephant seals and colonies of Emperor penguins with populations larger than most cities. Some of the world's greatest adventurers made their mark here too: Roald Amundsen, the first person to reach the South Pole on 14 December 1911; Scott's failed attempt that cost him his life; Shackleton's heroic journey home after his ship, the *Endurance*, became stuck in the ice.

But Antarctica is important for other reasons too. Glaciers, like the Lambert, are sensitive to small changes in temperature and act as a kind of early warning system for climate change, which is helping scientists gain a better grasp of its effects. By measuring them we can also gain a direct correlation with sea-level rises. And they are shrinking: 87 per cent of the Antarctic Peninsula's glaciers are currently in retreat. Deep within the ice, the Antarctic also holds one of the most complete records of climatic shifts on the planet, stretching back thousands of years. Ice cores taken from here are like photographs back in time, recording air temperature, chemistry and more. By literally looking into the depths of Antarctica itself, we can see our past and, maybe, help predict our future too.

And it's important that we do: 70 per cent of the planet's fresh water is contained within the Antarctic Ice Sheet. If it should melt, sea levels would rise 200 feet and drown the world's coasts. This may be one of the last frontiers of exploration on Earth, a frozen wilderness not fit for human life. But its silence and cold beauty calls to us, as it did to Amundsen, Scott and Shackleton, precisely because of that impossibility. And the secrets it holds are worth searching for still.

WHERE: Amery ice shelf, East Antarctica.

HOW TO SEE IT: The Lambert Glacier is in an extremely remote and hard to access location, so trips rarely pass by. But Antarctica itself has many options to explore. Almost everyone who visits is part of an organised cruise, 90 per cent of which depart from Ushuaia, Argentina, although there are a few trips that leave from ports in Australia and New Zealand too. Check out the International Association of Antarctica Tour Operators for a database of recommended operators, all of whom have been vetted for environmentally responsible Antarctic travel. The tour season runs November to March. December and January have relatively warmer temperatures, up to twenty hours of daily sunlight and the chance to see newborn penguin chicks. February and March have the best whale watching.
www.iaato.org

TOP TIPS: Book at least a year ahead for the best discounts. The lower decks are better for seasickness. Boats that hold

over 500 people are not allowed to land; smaller ships are often more expensive but can be a better experience.

TRY THIS INSTEAD: Greenland offers a wonderful polar experience. It usually costs less than a full Antarctic trip and, for most people, it's easier to reach too.
www.greenland.com

AURORA BOREALIS, ARCTIC CIRCLE

Witnessing the Aurora Borealis, or the Northern Lights as they're also known, is one of the most awe-inspiring experiences on the planet. Found in the Arctic Circle, around the tip of Siberia, Scandinavia, Iceland, Canada, Alaska and southern Greenland, this dazzling celestial spectacle is caused as particles from the sun interact with gases in the Earth's atmosphere. But the science is upstaged by the effect. Enormous curtains of colour sway in the night sky like ribbons of silk. Hues shift from light green to bright pink, rose, orange and blue. At points it is still, a wash of watercolour filling the immensity of the sky, and then it shimmers, dancing like waves on the night, receding to a thin line and stretching suddenly as far as the eye can see.

In the early 17th century, the astronomer Galileo gave them their name: Aurora, Roman goddess of the dawn, and Boreal, the Greek name for wind of the north. Descartes, Aristotle and Goethe refer to them in their writings. But their presence in human culture goes back much further: 30,000-year-old cave paintings depict the Aurora's swirling lights. Legends of their origin have been passed down by generation after generation of native people. But though their fascination is universal, we imprint something of ourselves in them too. In Norse mythology the lights were the armour of the Valkyries, leading fallen soldiers to Valhalla. The Menominee Indians of Wisconsin saw in them the torches of giants spear fishing at night. The indigenous people of the Arctic, the Inuit, saw spirits playing in the sky. Some were afraid: the Sami people hid indoors, the Chinese saw fire-breathing dragons and the Fox Indians thought it was their slain enemies preparing for revenge. But others welcomed them: fishermen in northern Sweden believed the lights were reflecting large schools of herring nearby; for the Cree Indians they were the spirits of their ancestors trying to communicate.

Science has its own story now too, of course. But although the truth may be more concrete, it is perhaps no less amazing. We are literally witnessing the energy of the sun itself. As the sun rotates on its axis, its magnetic fields interact and knot together to form sunspots. Eventually the intense magnetic energy from these regions explodes into solar flares and huge solar storms, called coronal mass ejections. These eruptions carry a shower of charged particles, electrons and ions, 93 million miles across space towards Earth. As they approach, they are drawn towards the planet's magnetic poles, in the same way as a bar magnet draws iron filings. Once they pass through the Earth's magnetic shield, they come into contact with atoms in the atmosphere. The type of gas molecule they come into contact with dictates the colours that we see: yellow and green for oxygen; red, violet and blue for nitrogen. The altitude affects the display too: for oxygen, we see green up to 150 miles high and red above; for nitrogen, we see blue up to 60 miles high and purple and violet above. When the solar flares are weak, they appear as a static band, when they are strong they dance across the sky in ever-changing rainbows of colour.

But although we may now be able to explain them scientifically, their effect on us is still unchanged. Whether we are witnessing the energy of the sun, the spirits of our ancestors or the gods looking down from heavenly fires above, it is much the same thing. There is something humbling and sublime in those ethereal lights. For there, among the stars, is a reflection of all that we feel but can't articulate or understand, a sense of transcendence, of hope and, perhaps, of something greater than ourselves.

WHERE: Most likely to be seen around the Arctic Circle, across the tip of Siberia, Scandinavia, Iceland, Canada, Alaska and southern Greenland. But can occasionally be seen further south.

HOW TO SEE IT: There are numerous tour operators, hotels and expert-led trips available; from dog-sledding adventures and wilderness camps to five-star hotels and Northern Lights cruises. Prime viewing season is October to March, though there are never any guarantees. Go to remote places, with the least light pollution, for the best chance. Usually sighted between 11pm and 2am.

TOP TIPS: Check the website below for real-time infor-mation on sun activity and probable Aurora viewing conditions around the world. If you can be flexible, wait for a coronal mass ejection to be reported (the explosion of super-charged particles from the sun), then go straight to a prime viewing location. When this solar wind sweeps by the Earth, one to three nights later, there is a good chance of excellent Aurora viewing.
www.swpc.noaa.gov/communities/space-weather-enthusiasts

TRY THIS INSTEAD: The Northern Lights are easier to spot, but the Southern Lights can be just as spectacular. Antarctica in the southern hemisphere winter, between May and September, offers the best chance. But if solar activity is strong, the lights can be seen in the South Island of New Zealand, southern Australia (especially Tasmania), southern Chile and Argentina, and very occasionally South Africa.

OUTER SPACE

THE INTERNATIONAL SPACE STATION, LOW EARTH ORBIT

The International Space Station (ISS) is one of humankind's greatest achievements. It is the largest and most complex structure ever flown in outer space and one of the most ambitious projects ever conceived in the history of the world. Right now, as you read this, a team of six astronauts is hurtling around the planet at 17,500 mph. They will complete a circle of the globe every 90 minutes, sixteen orbits a day, a sunrise or a sunset every 45 minutes. To date, the ISS has orbited the Earth more than 100,000 times.

Perhaps most impressively, it has been continuously manned since 2 November 2000. Most of the world's children alive today have never lived without a permanent settlement of people orbiting above them. The ISS, in this very real sense, is our first colony in space. And no country could have done it alone. Building it required the cooperation of a family of nations united in a single endeavour: to enrich the knowledge of all humankind and take our first steps towards our destiny in the stars.

Stretching 357 feet across, about the length of a football field, and weighing nearly 1 million pounds, it is the biggest object ever put in space. Attached to the centre truss are sixteen enormous solar panels, more than an acre across, and compartments where the crew work and live. There are no politics up here. Half of the station is run by America, half by Russia, with role of station commander alternating between the two countries, and astronauts from Canada, Japan and Europe regularly on board too.

For much of its early years, the crew were engaged in building the station itself. Components had to be flown up on rockets one at a time and then assembled, piece by piece, in orbit. This meant dozens of complex space walks each year, in which delicate engineering operations had to be performed in the vacuum of space. Each walk was potentially lethal and so had to be rehearsed in underwater simulators back on Earth for up to two years previously. That required an enormous logistical undertaking. And it's still ongoing. Supply ships must regularly drop food and materials, maintenance is constant and plans for expansion are in place.

But now that it's complete, its primary purpose is to do science. The microgravity environment on board enables a range of unique research opportunities, from developing new kinds of pharmaceuticals and combustion systems to collecting data about climate change, cosmic rays and dark matter. But perhaps most important of all is the work involved with studying the effects of space exploration on the human body. If the ISS is humanity's first step into outer space, the next is almost certainly Mars. But reaching the red planet would mean at least a two-year round trip. Aside from the psychological challenges, such an undertaking would exact an enormous toll on the human body. Even relatively short stints in zero-gravity result in astronauts losing significant amounts of bone and muscle mass, as well as other complications. Learning how to lessen these effects is vital to the future of long-term space exploration.

Astronauts on board today must counteract these physical side effects with a minimum of two and a half hours of exercise a day, six days a week. In between they are working flat out on maintenance, experiments, cleaning and repairs. They can't shower, they have to sleep tethered to a wall, eat vacuum-packed food and wear the same clothes for a week. It's hard work. But the payoff is they get to fly. Living in zero-gravity means being liberated from the laws of physics. Astronauts spend their three-, six- or even twelve-month-long quotas floating through the ship, utterly weightless, performing flips in mid-air. They describe it as sheer joy.

And then there's also that view. Looking at the Earth from space has had a profound, and often spiritual, effect on the few men and women lucky enough to see it. There is the exquisite beauty, of course: the dark blue oceans, storms of swirling white clouds, the faint line of turquoise and violet on the edge of the atmosphere, all the cities of man lighting up in the night. But more than that is what it all means. Almost without exception astronauts come home with a profound sense of humanity's shared destiny, that all the wars, all the conflicting ideologies, mean nothing when the Earth is viewed as it really is: a solitary sphere of life, alone in the vastness of space. Looking at the Earth from the outside there are no borders; the differences of race and nationality seem ludicrous, and the fragility of the Earth is more apparent than ever before.

That's the real wonder of the ISS. Not the science, the technology or the sheer achievement that it exists at all, but

the fact that it is the beginning, perhaps, of the next phase of humanity's story. And we did it together. Not one nation, but many, working together in peace to pursue our shared future in the stars.

WHERE: Low Earth orbit.

HOW TO SEE IT: It's possible to watch the ISS pass overhead from several thousand locations around the world. It appears as a fast moving star and can be seen easily with the naked eye.
http://spotthestation.nasa.gov

TOP TIP: Follow a live video feed from the ISS.
www.ustream.tv/channel/live-iss-stream

TRY THIS INSTEAD: Swiss Space Systems offer zero-gravity flights at various locations around the world. Participants experience the weightlessness of real astronauts on board a specially designed jumbo jet.
www.zerog.s-3.ch

SOLAR ECLIPSE

For as long as human beings have looked up at the sky, solar eclipses have terrified, amazed and filled us with dread and wonder. They are one of the world's most astonishing celestial events, a brief moment when the laws of nature are reversed and the darkness of night momentarily triumphs over the light of day.

For thousands of years they were shrouded in superstition. In ancient China, where the first eclipse was recorded on 22 October 2134 BC, they believed it was a dragon attempting to devour the sun. Astronomers who failed to predict them were promptly put to death. In Babylonia, eclipses were signs of the wrath of the gods. Astronomers there tried to predict them from at least 1375 BC so that substitute 'dummy' monarchs could be placed on the throne to try to misdirect their anger. They were written about in Homer's *The Odyssey*: 'the sun has perished out of heaven, and an evil mist hovers over all'. And mentioned in the Bible, the book of Amos 8:9: 'I will cause the sun to go down at noon, and I will darken the Earth in the clear day'. They have killed kings; Emperor Louis of Bavaria, the son of Charlemagne, was literally scared to death after witnessing an unusually long eclipse on 5 May 840. And they have stopped wars: the Lydians and Medes of ancient Greece threw down their weapons in 585 BC, seeing the dark skies as a sign to make peace.

They've also helped do some proper science. On 18 August 1868, French astronomer Pierre Janssen pointed his spectroscope at a few red dots hovering around the disc of the moon as it crossed the sun and discovered a new element: helium. On 29 May 1919, photographs of stars taken near the edge of the sun during a total eclipse were compared with photographs taken of the same region of sky at night, helping to prove Einstein's general theory of relativity, which predicted that the path of light would be warped by gravity.

But despite all their grandeur, solar eclipses are actually just an illusion caused by pure happenstance alone. In the phase of a new moon, when the lunar body moves to the side of the Earth facing the sun, it periodically lines up in such a way that the moon casts a shadow across the Earth. Because the moon's orbit is tilted, this occurs relatively infrequently.

But that it lines up so precisely at all is a mere fluke of celestial mechanics. The sun's 864,000-mile diameter is 400 times greater than the moon's. But the moon also happens to be just about 400 times closer to Earth than the sun, meaning that when their orbital planes intersect, we see the illusion of the moon appearing to completely cover it. But that won't always be so. Our lunar body is gradually moving away from the Earth at a rate of about 1.6 inches per year. In about a billion years, the illusion of solar eclipses will no longer occur.

The type of eclipse you see has to do with where you are and the way the moon's shadow is cast upon the Earth. In fact, there are two types of shadow. The umbra is a dark, narrow cone where all sunlight is blocked out. During an eclipse, as the Earth spins, this shadow races at 1,400 mph along a 100-mile wide corridor, called the path of totality. Anyone inside this zone will see a total eclipse, where the sun is completely covered by the moon and only the corona, the fiery outer atmosphere of the sun, remains. The penumbra is a wider band around the umbra, where sunlight is only partially obscured. In this zone, the moon only covers a segment of the sun; how much depends on how close you are to the central shadow. Most spectacular of all, many would say, is an annular eclipse. Here the moon is too small in its orbit to completely cover the sun, but still passes through it centrally, creating what looks like a burning ring of fire.

We know the science, but to see a solar eclipse first hand is no less dramatic and unsettling now than it was for our distant ancestors. Like them, a part of us is still unnerved by the sudden reversal of all that we have come to know and expect. Like them, we can't help but feel superstitious of the triumph of darkness, if only for an instant, over light.

WHERE: Locations vary.

HOW TO SEE IT: On average, a total eclipse occurs somewhere on Earth about every eighteen months. Partial eclipses are more common and usually occur a few times a year. Check NASA's website for detailed predictions.
http://eclipse.gsfc.nasa.gov/eclipse.html

TOP TIPS: Observing a solar eclipse directly is very dangerous. The safest option is to build a pinhole camera and observe the eclipse projected onto a screen placed roughly three feet behind it. Sunglasses are not strong enough to protect your eyes.

TRY THIS INSTEAD: A lunar eclipse is when Earth's shadow is cast onto the moon. The most spectacular version is known as a blood-red moon, the equivalent of a total solar eclipse, when the lunar body is in complete shadow and all that can be seen is the red glow of the planet's sunrises and sunsets reflected onto the moon's surface. Check NASA's website for detailed predictions.
http://eclipse.gsfc.nasa.gov/lunar.html

THE MILKY WAY

There is, perhaps, no greater wonder of the world than simply looking up at the stars. On a clear night, surrounded in darkness, the Milky Way appears as a living thing: a swirling mass of luminescent lights and astral clouds breathing in the blackness with eyes of pure white fire. It's no surprise our ancient ancestors saw gods and demons and dragons with silver skin above. They lived out here, under the stars. The sky was their blanket. Every time we look up at the twinkling of night we share something of that history with them. We feel those gods still, in that great unknown. Surely there is some purpose to all this, we think, some future not yet revealed. Surely we are not alone. And yet the more we learn, the more science kills the gods of old, the more those gods return in ever-deepening mysteries and new questions and concepts we can barely understand.

The Milky Way, our home, is a barred spiral galaxy, 100,000 light years across. Four arms curl around its centre, like a starfish bending in the wind, each one 1,000 light years thick, spinning around a supermassive black hole at its heart. Our solar system is a speck of light on the far reaches of the galaxy. When we look up and see that milky river of stars, like a smudge of silver across the night sky, we are actually looking into the centre of the Milky Way from the outer edge of one of its wings, 25,000 light years away.

But the real wonder of the stars is the moment when all this becomes real. Right now, this instant, the Earth is moving through space at 66,000 mph. In the time it will take you to read this chapter, you will have travelled more than 5,000 miles. For real: you would have actually, physically travelled that distance through space. Add on the fact that the solar system itself is spinning on the arms of the Milky Way at a rate of roughly 330 miles per second and that number is closer to 100,000 miles.

And then there is just the sheer number of stars. On the clearest of nights we can see a few thousand. But in our galaxy alone there are more than 200 billion. To put that number in perspective, if you stacked 200 billion dollar bills one on top of the other, it would reach more than twenty times the height of Mount Everest. Now imagine each of those stars again as a grain of salt. Pour them out into a room around you and you would be covered to the neck. Pick up a single grain. That's our sun. Our entire solar system, every great leader, thought, work of art, piece of music, friend and lover you've ever had is floating around that microscopic grain, too small to see with the naked eye.

And we are but one galaxy among billions. The latest supercomputer simulations estimate there are 500 billion galaxies in the universe. Not stars, entire galaxies, each one filled with hundreds of billions of stars, and each of those with planets, moons and, maybe, worlds just like ours. If we only count suns that are the same size as ours, and planets the same distance away from the sun as Earth, in our galaxy alone there are more than 8 billion potentially habitable worlds. Look up: the chance that we are alone is infinitely smaller than the chance that we are not.

And there's so much we still don't know. Scientists believe 90 per cent of our universe is made of dark matter, but no one knows exactly what it is or how to find it. Our universe could be composed of vibrating strings of energy or bubbles of space-time. And then there's us. Current theories, real science, suggest that our consciousness is inextricably linked to the creation of reality. That when we look at the stars, we are not just seeing fiery distant lights; we are somehow an essential part of making those stars real. Our minds summon the universe into existence, like a dream we all share.

That's why looking up at the stars is the greatest wonder of all. Because the more we know, the more mysteries are revealed. Because they make us feel infinitesimally small, but part of something incomprehensibly large. There are ten times more stars in the universe than there are grains of sand in all the beaches and deserts of the world. We are

Photo: Q-lieb-in

made of stardust. The cosmos is not just out there; it is in us too. And we feel a part of that awe, that magnificence, every time we look up. And that's what wonder is all about.

WHERE: Above you right now.

HOW TO SEE IT: Dark sky preserves are designated areas where no light pollution is allowed. There are dozens throughout the world and they offer some of the best stargazing on the planet. Go online to find a dark sky area near you.
www.darksky.org

TOP TIP: Time your visit with a new moon for the best viewing conditions.

TRY THIS INSTEAD: The Atacama Desert in Chile is recognised as one of the best stargazing locations in the world. Numerous tour operators offer expert-led, specialist trips to the region.
www.chile.travel/en